"Major Opportunities"

The Door is Wide Open

David Slaughter

authorHOUSE

AuthorHouse™ LLC
1663 Liberty Drive
Bloomington, IN 47403
www.authorhouse.com
Phone: 1-800-839-8640

© 2013 by David Slaughter. All rights reserved.

No part of this book may be reproduced, stored in a retrieval system, or transmitted by any means without the written permission of the author.

Published by AuthorHouse   08/22/2013

ISBN: 978-1-4918-0521-3 (sc)
ISBN: 978-1-4918-0522-0 (hc)
ISBN: 978-1-4918-0523-7 (e)

Library of Congress Control Number: 2013913875

Any people depicted in stock imagery provided by Thinkstock are models, and such images are being used for illustrative purposes only.
Certain stock imagery © Thinkstock.

This book is printed on acid-free paper.

Because of the dynamic nature of the Internet, any web addresses or links contained in this book may have changed since publication and may no longer be valid. The views expressed in this work are solely those of the author and do not necessarily reflect the views of the publisher, and the publisher hereby disclaims any responsibility for them.

Dedicated to:

To Ma Ma: Thank you for being my mentor, my source of inspiration, for always seeing the best in me and for the consistent praise and love you provided unconditionally.

To Reese Dennis: Thank you or showing me through example in your short span of 18 years that y being the best you can be, you can be the very best you should be.

To Steve: Thank you   showing me through your pain and perseverance and through your   ple as a brother what it is like to walk a tough road, yet manage eep your head high.

To My five c   n-I Love You.

~ Table of Contents ~

The Door of Opportunity is <u>Wide Open!</u>... ix

Chapter 1: Major Opportunity at UHD.. 1

Chapter 2: One Door Leads to Another 21

Chapter 3: All you have to do is Ask... 28

Chapter 4: Opening the Right Door... 48

Chapter 5: Mentoring 101: Learning & Teaching 67

Chapter 6: Major Opportunities Require Change 91

Chapter 7: In Tragedy or Crisis-Major Opportunities
May Arise!.. 108

Chapter 8: Brainstorming 101: Finding Opportunities 120

Chapter 9: The Seven Building Blocks of Major Opportunity...138
1. Interviewing for Keeps... 141
2. Hiring the Best... 148
3. Training them to Stay 150
4. Counseling to Improve Performance 152
5. Motivation 101: Doing it through others............................ 156
6. Writing-Conducting Effective Annual Reviews................ 163
7. Terminations & Separations -with Dignity 164

Chapter 10: Major Opportunities to Succeed 167
- A Vision of Success, Begins Early! 167
- What makes Me Successful? 168
- Goal setting & Means of Measure 169
- Becoming obsessed with numbers! 170
- Finding Balance in life — in the Middle! 174

Chapter 11: Getting Them to Come Back,
          By Getting Them to Stay 178

Chapter 12: Major Opportunities, to Pass It On 191
- Treating people right 192
- It always comes back to you! 192
- Find your Major Opportunity to pass it on! 198

Chapter 13: Major Opportunity Success Stories 205

"Major Opportunities"
The Door of Opportunity is <u>Wide Open</u>!

  The title of this book finalized as I completed my long sought after undergraduate degree at the University of Houston-Downtown. "Major Opportunities," is about much more than an advertising launch for a major university in Houston, Texas that I am actively involved in promoting. The term encompasses daily challenges we face and the opportunities that arise in life. Doors of opportunity open due to one's ability to achieve what they put their mind to when they do their very best. In the highly competitive, technologically driven, fast-paced world we live in, it requires a solid plan of action to turn challenges and obstacles into "Major Opportunities."

  There is always the possibility of one overlooking or ignoring doors of opportunities that can open. These doors are symbolic of one's perspective of the past, it presents an opportunity to examine the present, and it represents a door of vision into the future. Doors of success open in order to maximize one's potential. Many doors simply require a knock to gain entry but often, one must peek inside a slightly open door, carefully and deliberately, all the while shadowing an opportunity with cautious optimism. On occasion, doors of opportunity are obscure from sight and many times one will discover that one door may lead to another. Occasionally, one may become lost, confused or disoriented perhaps even forgetting which door they came through to begin with. All in all, persistence is our greatest asset when it comes to opening new doors into the future. The doors I reference remain emblematic of life's prospects and represent one's opportunity to pursue their true passion in life.

Doors of "Major Opportunities," are <u>wide open</u> from the minute we wake up in the morning and take our first breath until we retire for rest at the end of a long day, anxiously awaiting the next new opportunity to explore. They open with our first phone conversation, with the first person we see or talk to but always, with our first contact with the real world. They continue to remain accessible all day on our journey to experience exposure to vibrant, exciting people, all of which have an ability to help open doors. As we will discover, these doors offer a way to understand and apply the meaning of life, while providing a vehicle of fun, reward and intrigue. To appreciate life as an opportunity to succeed we must test the handles of a door in search of one's master plan. "Major Opportunities," exist in both our personal lives and in our career path. I trust that this book can serve as a catalyst to examine, assess, restore, and refresh our perspective in search of success and inner peace achieved by walking through open doors. By sharing this book, one of my goals is that you too can find a lighted path to assist you as you move swiftly towards "Major Opportunities," waiting on you.

Life is short my friends and waiting for doors to magically open I fear, places us in peril of being left with lingering, important, unanswered questions we might gather along the way. A danger may exist placing us at risk in later years left speculating about matters left undone, wondering about dreams unimagined and unopened doors. Just in case you need additional motivation to knock on the doors revealed behind the pages of this book, here are some reasons this book might also open a door for you.

- If you did not finish college, yet desire to obtain a degree
- If you enjoy stories, analogies and anecdotes about success
- If you want to learn how to overcome objections
- If you seek to understand and apply mentoring skills

- If you want to learn how to succeed by leading others
- If you seek to motivate others to their highest potential
- If you are in sales and desire to move into management
- If you desire to control the results in your career consistently
- If you desire to improve upon methods to open and close sales
- If you have experienced a crisis or a tragedy in your life
- If you want to stop and pursue your true passion in life
- If you want to incorporate your life's work with pride
- If you face change, but you do not know how to embrace it
- If you want to learn to turn "no" into "yes," more often

It is important to me that this book is inspirational and motivational to my readers. It is my fervent hope that you will find a way by reading this message to improve your life situation and that principles shared might promote healthy changes in your world of thought, actions and deeds. I trust that by describing deliberate, purposeful, proven ways to find new doors to explore new opportunities will appear that you did not know existed. As you read this true to life story, a personal expectation I have is that you will become cognizant of a healthier way by which you may take advantage of life's "Major Opportunities." My promise to you is that these doors are wide open and that they can aid you in your personal endeavor to climb "Mount Success."

Let me take you through a door that opened for me!

~ Chapter 1 ~
"Major Opportunity" at UHD

Today is November 9, 2012, a great day to remember. It offers a path of study as we begin our journey together, seeking to explore the "Major Opportunities" that exist in life for each of us in our careers and in our personal lives. It was the kind of day that can help assemble the pieces in this complicated puzzle of life, assisting one to find acknowledgement that there are doors of opportunities all around us. It was the kind of day on which super bowls have been played, a day capable of supplying one with the inner strength, the courage, the excitement and the vision to believe that—for one split second-one really can fly.

At 7:45 a.m. on this day, I arrived at the Junior League of Houston, a wonderful facility located near the Houston Galleria. Even though I have lived in Houston much of my life, I had not been in this building since my brother in law's wedding, which seems like so many years ago now. It was a beautiful morning, no clouds in the sky, lots of sun and I had a special hitch in my step as I left my car in the parking garage and hurriedly entered the building. The University of Houston-Downtown's (UHD) President's Community Breakfast was an invitation only event in which the president of UHD invited individuals to attend with a primary goal of providing an update of past and current university successes; offering insight into the future of the school's growth; and information regarding long term planning.

More than two hundred people attended the event, including Houston Councilman Ed Gonzales, UHD alumni, donors, supporters and local businessmen and women, all who came to hear Dr. Flores present a vision for the future. Six of UHD's nine "Major Opportunity" students, selected as building blocks of a new marketing campaign launched in spring 2012, also attended the event. As I walked into the room I passed a huge sign with a picture of these students that read, "UHD President's Community Breakfast: Inspiring Success." The fact that UHD sees each of us as inspiring success made this a special day to be a part of right from the beginning.

Quickly, I realized this was more than just a community breakfast. It was clear that the nine of us are students of which UHD is very proud. It was something I fathomed when we went to a photo shoot prior to the launch of the campaign. I confirmed it as well with our pictures plastered on billboards, banners and advertising materials dispersed to the community, even placed upon the walls of the university. It was validated once again as I walked into the assembly for breakfast that morning, seeing five of us on a screen in the large room, a picture to remain visible for the entire morning. When handed a tag "Table Host," a big light came on, it was show time for UHD's honored students and the pride I felt must have lit me up like a Roman candle. Surely, the light must have blinded some of those around me.

What I did not know was how true it is that UHD is a university with more vision than the competition. What I did not know is how much more love I was capable of feeling for my university when I left, than when I arrived. What I did not know is how special we would feel in front of community members, faculty and staff. It was as though we were the light, symbolic of the desires, goals and successes that one may achieve at a great university by one who seeks an opportunity. The program read, "UHD: Major Opportunities on the Horizon."

The Junior League of Houston
Photo Courtesy of John Everett
(Pictured Dr. William Flores)

What I confirmed that morning is how fortunate UHD is to have an incredible university president with a passion for students unlike any I have seen in a college president. During the event, I learned more about the talent and the class of the other five major opportunity students that attended. Prior to this, I knew them only from a distance through indirect exposure to the same program for which we represented. What I confirmed, is something I noticed during the first semester I attended the school—that UHD is great because the people who work there are great. They are committed to their profession but mostly, they are committed to "excellence."

Commitment to excellence starts at the very top I have learned, and UHD is no exception to that rule. I remember what I learned while running a retail company in the private sector, which equally applies to receiving an education in the public sector. That is, without exception, the people in any school, organization or company are the ones that provide the building blocks for success. One of the highlights of the morning was hearing from A'Tondra Gilstrap, a current UHD student from the Scholars Academy in the College of Sciences and Technology. Her story was inspiring to all of us. It occupies a place in the final chapter of this book, as I share her compelling story in detail in chapter thirteen, "Major Opportunity Success Stories." She is an example of one of the high-potential students about whom UHD can brag and she is just one of the 14, 000 remarkable students at the University of Houston-Downtown, all seeking "Major Opportunities."

The Junior League of Houston
Photo Courtesy of John Everett

As I observed the other five UHD student-representatives interact with guests during the event I noticed that every one of them was doing what they do best-engaging in conversation with person after person, gaining insight and perspective from those who surrounded them from the Houston community. Students who care about their education seize opportunities available and they use their experiences as a way to connect with others. I made it a point to tell Dr. Flores how proud he made me feel of UHD, how special he made all of us feel. I praised him for a special award he recently received. Blushing, UHD leader's response was, "Give the recognition to the students, they make the university what it is, they make UHD great." Dr. Flores, the consummate UHD promoter and unselfish man he is, was directing attention away from himself toward students in his typical fashion. A devout leader at the top of any organization sets the standard for the entire team and Dr. William Flores demonstrates he is a dedicated leader. What I know now more than ever is that I love the University of Houston-Downtown and he does too.

At the close of the event, there were pictures taken, meaningful conversations and new friends to become acquainted with. I found myself as one of the last to leave the facility, wanting to linger to savor the meaningful moment UHD had given us. With adrenaline pulsing through my veins, I walked out of the room and headed back into the world with new eyes, a renewed spirit and a thirsty desire to drink the water UHD has to offer its students, called major opportunity. I made the comment as I was walking out to an administrator, "How could the rest of the day top that?" He smiled at me and said, "It was a great experience, wasn't it?" With my heart pumping and my blood rushing, I headed back to my car thinking, "Today is the first day of the rest of my life."

The Junior League of Houston
Photo Courtesy of John Everett

"Major Opportunities"

It seems necessary to retrace my steps prior to attending this incredible event. As I reflect upon the significance of what led up to this day, it may help us piece a puzzle together. A puzzle that serves as a model reflecting opportunities we may find. Going back to complete your college degree at 53 is no easy task. For that matter, it is a daunting task at any age when one has not participated in the educational experience for so long. I suspect that some of us, perhaps many of us, secretly have a desire to do what I am doing, but lack the time, the confidence or the opportunity to accomplish it. I say definitively that you can do it, that anyone can do it. You simply have to walk through a door called, "Higher Education," and it is always wide open. You need to make that first call, make a visit to a college campus or, inquire online. It may seem scary or it may appear hidden as an opportunity, but it is a door that has to be knocked on to open. A college degree is not outside the realm of possibility for any person, at any age, in any occupation.

At the risk of digressing for the remainder of the book, I need to fill you in on my story. In October 2007, I resigned from the one and only company I worked for since my initial college days. During the twenty-four years I worked for Stage Stores Inc. in Houston, Texas, from 1983 until 2007, my experiences were fun, fruitful, and rewarding, something I would expect from a first class, thriving organization. It was a top of the mountain experience for all of those years. The mentors I had the privilege of knowing, the people I worked with and the results I reaped created memories of a lifetime.

After departing my position at Stage Stores Inc., I rested, read, traveled and played for a few years, which I highly recommend during one's mid-life if it is possible. Call it a break, a rest, call it seeing your kids, a "middle-age crisis," call it what you want as it was good. Spending time with family without the interference and interruptions of work was refreshing. I decided in June 2011 that I wanted to go back to school to complete the college degree I suspect many assumed I had all along. I conducted some deliberate research into my opportunities. I began by visiting with

Houston Baptist University (HBU), the same university where I had squandered precious time in my youth while enjoying a free ride via a full debate scholarship for three years in the 80s. It was a university where my effort may have been excused all too often for physical absence in exchange for a contribution in debate trophies. I did not apply myself and as a result, I received the average grades that I truly deserved.

Incidentally, HBU is a great institution on so many levels. The blame, the wasted time, and the incompleteness rest on my shoulders. Next, I went by the University of Houston main campus and had an informative interview with admissions on the spot, seeing a beautiful spread-out campus, leaving with an open door to walk through should I choose to do so. It was an impressive visit and it is a strong university. I also went by Rice University just for good measure, as I just love that campus. After all, what is there not to love about Rice University?

Then, my son Christopher suggested that I consider the school he attended, the University of Houston-Downtown. He told me what he liked was the affordability factor, the smaller class size and that his professors were outstanding. I listened to Chris and I did indeed check out UHD, first on line and then in person. In all the years I have lived in Houston, I had not visited their campus and I discovered quickly that it might be the best-kept secret on the bayou.

From the minute I applied to UHD, through registration, through the admission process, through an often-tedious financial aid process, it was clear that UHD was ready and willing to help me succeed this time should I choose to take advantage of the opportunity. Perhaps what stood out most were the prevailing positive attitudes, the helpful can-do people, the "I can" and "I will," answers from employees at UHD. I found this attitude to be prevalent throughout the university during my transitional period and through subsequent semesters. It is easy to understand why the UHD student body population has grown to over 14,000 with an 8% increase in 2012, and it is because of an intense desire to be "excellent."

"Major Opportunities"

As I said, going back to school at 53 is not a simple decision. Frankly, it came as no great disappointment to me in August 2011, when I received a letter from the University of Houston main campus stating that they were sorry, too much time had now lapsed, that my offer to attend was no longer on the table. They were correct; the offer had been tabled, but by me. For you see, I had chosen my school and it was the University of Houston-Downtown. That is not to suggest that everything was perfect from that moment until my graduation in May 2013. There are always adjustments and surprises; certainly, there is an expected learning curve in going back to school after many years, but UHD made it easy for me to take advantage of the opportunity.

I made a commitment to get you caught up to this point in my 55 years so we have to continue to reverse our course for a while longer. In keeping with the title of this chapter, "Major Opportunity at UHD," I want to describe a trail of events, opportunities and doors that opened for me, the same ones that can open for anyone who knocks at the door. Three things happened my first semester back in school that I want to share with you.

Major Opportunity # 1 at UHD

My first major opportunity at UHD came when I signed up for a class that my son recommended taught by Dr. Vida Robertson, associate professor of English. Chris told me he was one of the best teachers he had ever had. I now understand, three semesters later why he made that comment and he was right. One of my English teachers had told me at Bellaire High School that I was a C writer. Although I excelled in debate and competitive sports, she implied I was just an average writer. "Some people just can't write," she said bluntly, and yet, she was so very wrong.

From the first day of class, it was clear that Dr. Robertson was unique, demanding and unwilling to lower his standards for any one of us. He was somewhat intimidating due to his scholarly manner and his vocabulary that left many hanging on his words, grasping to connect the intellectual dots to form complete sentences. This sophomore English literature class focused on African American studies, a new subject matter for me. The class was void of seniors and included a mix of freshmen, sophomores and a few of us older folks. He made it clear that we could expect quizzes often over the literature assigned to read according to the syllabus and as it would turn out, he would remain painfully true to his word.

Apparently, it was no great task for Dr. Robertson to verify if we had read our assignments or not as this was not his first time with the material, he told us. So when our class discussion began and we had a "deer in the headlights" look, it did not take him long to spot a bunch of fakes, relying upon one or two students that actually completed the assigned reading those first few weeks. In one of the classes early on, it must have been clear that we were unprepared for a discussion and so he decided to talk to us about us In my case, I was doing the weekly reading but I was confused, perhaps lost in translation as the lingo was not one I was accustomed to. It was difficult for me to seem as intelligent as my business acumen suggested I might be.

During this class, he stopped suddenly, seemingly out of frustration and spent the remainder of that period talking about our education, our goals and our desire to learn. Dr. Robertson explained to us that whether we were students at UHD, Rice, or Harvard, for that matter, any university of higher learning, we were there to receive and were paying for an education commensurate with excellence. He was unwilling to compromise that philosophy by watering down his curriculum, his expectations or his pursuit of excellence in order to accommodate our lack of study time and preparation for class participation. The room became unusually quiet and we were now listening attentively to what he was saying.

That day a light came on for many of us, as Dr. Robertson was determined in his purpose to make his point by deliberately interrupting the class. The light he turned on was now shining blindly in my eyes. It was the exact same light I had turned off years ago when awarded grades I did not deserve, causing me to be an under-achiever on my accord. I remember being the first student that spoke up as he finally stopped lecturing us, as it got quieter, as he looked at us and concluded his oration by saying, "Well, what do you have to say students of English literature?" It seemed he was prepared to wait for questions, answers or denials for as long as it took.

Bravely, I said "Dr. Robertson, to be honest with you, I am struggling with the nature of the literature, but I am thrilled you have set high expectations for all of us." I explained passionately as I recall that it felt as though I was short-changed during my first foray in college. Without hesitation I said, "I did not earn the high marks I was capable of due to a complete and total lack of effort on my part." I admitted openly that I had not done myself any favors milking the process the first time round. I proclaimed apologetically, "Shame on me, and shame on those professors for giving me grades I did not deserve. I cheated me, and so did they, I want to be challenged, I do not want to be cheated and I am not going to cheat myself anymore."

Amazingly, other lights appeared to brighten the room as well as some of us began to assume some level of accountability. Another student raised her hand and explained that she might have lost out because some of her high school experience. A second student spoke up, revealing some of the same experiences, saying she too believed that the system had failed her, that perhaps she had taken advantage of the system too. A few more students jumped in to become part of the dialog as it appeared we were making excuses, pointing the blame at a broken educational system. At least we were talking and thinking and from Dr. Robertson's perspective, we were now engaged in the conversation. It was clear to all of us we were participating in a real discussion and that perhaps we were now ready to participate. Judging by the smile on his face, perhaps he could now do what he was there to accomplish, to teach those who want to learn.

From that day forward, almost everyone began reading their assignments and the weekly quiz scores validated that fact. Most importantly, our minds were wide open and we were ready to receive the quality instruction for which we were paying, the one Dr. Robertson had promised to deliver. We began meeting and bonding in small study groups outside of class and that continued throughout the semester. By the way, all of the papers I wrote were not C papers; they were well-written, well-argued and well-researched. He offered us several opportunities to earn extra credit and I took advantage of every extra-credit point I could. The mid-term in Dr. Robertson's class was the second-hardest test I have taken and the final was the hardest test I have taken, but I made an A in the class and I did it the old-fashioned way, I earned it. It should come as no surprise to you that I signed up for another of Dr. Robertson's classes the following semester as well, which I thoroughly enjoyed too.

Major Opportunity #2 at UHD

Major opportunity number two that semester came about after I enrolled in a microbiology class taught by Dr. Poonam Gulati. Frankly, taking math or science was like facing my worst fear, next to eating spinach or anything green. It is hard to believe that I could oversee 200 retail stores with $450 million in annual sales, yet math and science were a struggle for me since I was 16 but I suspect I am not the only one in that boat. I wanted A's this time around and I certainly did not want a single C, as that would defeat the purpose of going back to college. I was not looking for a piece of paper this time around. Instead, I was seeking an opportunity to make the Dean's list.

About half-way through the semester, faced with my second major test in microbiology, I would experience my first big challenge. I never missed a single class that semester, but the material in this science class was no longer sticking and I panicked so I decided I needed a new strategy. The day before the second test, I went with a friend to an event at a private school. I purchased a butter crème cake wrapped in Halloween wrapping for $20, it looked scrumptious and I had planned to eat it. When I got home though, I knew that the last thing I needed to do was to consume all 15 pounds of a butter cake, which I could easily have swallowed in one bite. Instead, a little light went off in my head and I typed a cute note and taped it to the outside wrapping. I addressed it from our microbiology class as it read, "Here's something sweet to sweeten your day, Dr. Gulati, signed, your sweet microbiology class." A positive plan of action is indeed a strategy for success even when it means a butter crème cake might be the only way out.

The next day, fearful of a mindboggling test, but not in an effort to bribe, I walked into the hallway with this beautiful wrapped cake in hand with note attached. The other students were waiting in the hall as usual, many still studying, as maybe I should have been. One of them said, "What is that?" I said, "It's a cake for Dr. Gulati from all of us." They looked at me, then some smiled, several high-fived me, but there were no cheers as I might have expected. As Dr. Gulati arrived and we went inside, I handed her the cake. She had no real immediate physical response. I sense she was in her test mode as we began to take the test almost immediately, which was not a good thing for me. Since never intended to be a bribe, her lack of response to the cake had no net impact upon my psyche as she passed out David's soon to be test of death.

As I began to examine the test closely, I realized I was in trouble — I mean real trouble. I knew quickly that an F was a definite possibility and the nausea that over took me should have been a legitimate reason to be excused from the test. No curve could alter the impending disaster I was facing. No offering of a butter crème cake could sweeten this pot. For a moment, I considered taking my cake and leaving, but my better instincts took over and tied me to the lab chair I was assigned early in the semester. Finishing the test in record time, reluctantly, I turned it in and I knew I was moving in the wrong direction of the Dean's list with two more tests ahead. I now faced losing confidence in my ability to understand the material but mainly I was looking a dreaded C straight in the face, cake or no cake.

Frustrated with only myself, I went straight home and composed an email. First, I sent it to God with no immediate response and then I forwarded it to Dr. Gulati, the one person who might understand my concern and perhaps reduce my sense of panic. I stated in the email that I was confused, embarrassed and frustrated and that I had studied my brains out but if I received a 50, I would be shocked. I indicated to her that I am not a quitter, that I will not fail and I refuse to drop her class. I asked if there might be extra credit or anything I could do in order to reverse the direction I was traveling. I considered asking if I could wash her car but I deferred to better judgment, protecting what little pride I had left in my ability to master the world of science. Dr. Gulati then demonstrated by her reaction what distinguishes her as a GREAT professor when she responded as quickly as she always does. Her response was for me not to fear, she appreciated my commitment to her class and that she would look into whether or not a curve might apply. Most importantly, she said, "Do not give up David!" and she added, "The cake is very good."

Within minutes, I had been shown empathy, compassion, and offered hope all at the same time by a seemingly unemotional, analytical science professor. "Perhaps mercy was to follow," I thought to myself. The respect she earned from me that day was immeasurable. I understand why her name and picture is on a frame on the wall of fame at UHD, noted as a distinguished professor at UHD. It validated that there are opportunities in the most challenging of circumstances as I knocked on a door of an opportunity to succeed. I received a whopping 66 on my nightmare rollercoaster of intellectual pursuit, otherwise known as a microbiology test. Doors of major opportunity do not always start out looking like they are the right door to enter, but one can change that by going through a different door or by looking for a door out and I chose to stay inside the door.

Do not misinterpret the point I am making as Dr. Gulati did not relax testing methods over the material going forward, that is clearly not her style, but she did allow us a major opportunity for extra credit. Some chose to do it and some did not. My extra credit was a model of a human cell. My daughter Madison and I worked on it together and the time spent was worth more than the extra points earned, as it was great father-daughter time and getting that with a seventeen year old is not easy. My daughter observed her dad as being someone that is willing to do the work necessary to achieve the best he could in life.

The next test I received an 89 with a lot of study and preparation time and some prayer, but no cake was required this time. Ultimately, I earned a B in her class, which was my only B earned at UHD, but I am very proud of that B as it contributed to my final 3.92 GPA. The lessons gained are worth remembering and is one of the important messages of this book as I validated that great professors have merciful and caring hearts and they have a role in the doors of opportunity that remain open. I also proved to myself that you can earn whatever grades you want, even as a student at age 53, if you make the effort and I was reminded of the main reason I chose UHD, because of great professors like Dr. Poonam Gulati. I still stop by and see her sometimes, as her door is always wide open for me and I know I have a friend, a mentor and a confidant for life.

While completing this manuscript, several times over 12 months of writing I was compelled to add to, elaborate or extend upon a story. For example, today I attended an awards ceremony in which Dr. Gulati received the UHD service award. It recognizes one professor at UHD as the best. With pride, admiration and honor, I watched as this humble, caring, brilliant professor accepted her award and this day, her success—was my success and her door—was my door.

Success in microbiology had more to do with my desire to succeed, with an effort to do the work and with my commitment to fight until the bitter-end relentlessly and defined by a willingness to walk through a door of opportunity rather than seeing it as a locked door. A lack of "best" effort as a student, an employee, a parent, as a son or a daughter, a spouse, as whomever you are always has a direct impact upon the end result you desire to achieve.

I refer to the "Doors of Major Opportunity" throughout this book as doors that must be knocked on, walked into and explored. My grandmother, an endearing, giving, loving Christian woman, was a mentor to me. She taught me something when I was young that I have tried to apply consistently, something I have not forgotten. In fact, I recited it again to 18,000 people in my keynote commencement speech at graduation on May 18, 2013. She kept a poem framed and placed on a wall in her home that read, "If a task is once begun, never leave it 'til it's done, be the labor, great or small, do it well or not at all." Doing it well requires doing it to the best of one's ability and Ma Ma, this time I did it very well.

Likewise, my mom also provided encouragement to me, bundled in a slightly sobering, real-life analogy. In a reference to my family responsibility of getting the trash to the curb, one I had been shirking as of late, she offered sound advice. She said, "David, you have three options as I see it. First, you can do it to the very best of your ability; second, you can do it and complain all the way, as you have been doing; or third, you can choose not to do it. "Two of those options have negative consequences," she said and "I will let you figure out which ones those are." My response in early debate prep mode was, "Well, what if I just delegate it?" No response was necessary, only that motherly look of discontent, reflecting a slightly irreverent disconnect on my part pertaining to the deeper more meaningful analogy she was providing. Truthfully, my mom and Ma Ma wanted the same thing for me; they wanted me to apply my very best effort and accept the result or the consequence deserved or earned. This philosophy if followed consistently can enable anyone to succeed at a high level, simply by giving a best effort.

"Major Opportunities" are discovered by exploring new doors with great anticipation and with enthusiasm. The opportunity, the success to enjoy and those doors will be ones that you must seek out for yourself. You will find that most often doors of opportunity are linked directly to the effort you make each day to open them. Success is not measured by how you do versus others, success is measured by how you do versus what YOU are capable of. Recently, my youngest daughter Ellie and I were heading to softball tryouts. Last season, she played competitively for the first time and she headed home from the first day of practice saying, "So Daddy, these are my arms and my legs and if I move them faster, I will go faster?" Ellie did not know how to hold a bat at her first practice, yet later, I observed her taking her turn in the batting cage, gripping that same bat as if was now too light for her, as if it might just break the bat if she hit that poor little softball. I refer to that as confidence and it has to do with knowing you gave your best in softball, in relationships and in life.

As we drove to her tryouts this second season with slightly higher expectations for both of us, she expressed some concerns. She said, "Daddy, there are so many who are better than me." I found myself repeating a life lesson to her as I said in the best Zig Ziglar voice I could muster, "Ellie, sweetie, always remember that success is not measured by how you do against others, it is measured based on your own capabilities and you are capable of much." She smiled, was selected and we have never looked back. Success is dependent upon you, your effort and your personal commitment to do the very best you can do. As I attended games this season, I watched as Eleanor drew back her bat back each time she stepped up to the plate, always looking over at me with a smile that communicated silently, "I'm gonna smack that ball Daddy, watch me hit it." I understand that when she smiles she desires to do the best she can do, and that is all I expect as her father. Recently, at the end of her second season, I had an opportunity to speak with her coach at a practice. I recounted how much she loves her team, her coaches and how much I could see her confidence growing every practice and from game to game. I told him how impressed I was with his personal style, one focused upon positive, encouragement, recognition—but founded upon love. "A great coach wears many hats," I told him. I wanted him to know that he wears them very well.

Major Opportunity #3 at UHD

Major opportunity number three occurred near the end of the first semester. It provides another example of the major opportunities that exist and validates that doors can open at any moment, if you knock on them. I read an article published in UHD Dateline, the student newspaper, it was an article written by some young man, let us call him, "Mr. Smith." The article was entitled, "What one ex UHD Student Thinks UHD Needs." It began by recounting that "Mr. Smith" had attended UHD for four semesters and he just knew there were great things about the school and then he proceeded to say what was wrong, what ought to be changed "Perhaps even change the name," he politely suggested. Inflamed at his apparent ignorance, I knew that I had to write a response.

The ex-debater in me demanded a rebuttal so I wrote an article entitled, "What One Current UHD Student Thinks UHD Has!" I had not written for a newspaper since high school but I was smart enough to run a large company, smart enough to write training programs, recognition programs, charge solicitation programs, smart enough to prepare district manager meetings and store manager meetings, so why not a simple rebuttal to an article not well thought out.

In the article, I explained who I was, where I came from, why I was here and what I loved about my experience so far at UHD, the antithesis of "Mr. Smith's" article. I described my personal experience with professors like Dr. Robertson and Dr. Gulati in vivid detail as I defended all that is great at UHD and I concluded by suggesting that perhaps students need to wake up and smell the roses. Despite my training and all of the techniques acquired as an executive to accomplish what I wanted, this time, I did not get my way as the editor chose not to publish the article. Instead, she explained that when she took the I's and the ME's out of the piece, there was simply nothing left to print. She said a good writer leaves everything about himself or herself out of an article typically; otherwise, it is not objective for a reader. "Really?" I thought to myself. I suspect she missed the point altogether, as I was freely offering years of expertise, experience and wisdom acquired through mistakes and success as a way to prove that "Mr. Smith," was wrong and he was! I did notice a new editor the following semester with a new staff and by the way, I have written six articles since, and all of them, published.

Even though my rebuttal was dead on arrival, I had acted based upon executive instinct and centered upon what my half-full glass perspective has always told me to do. When I submitted the article to the editor, I also forwarded it to the president of the university, Dr. Flores, with a note, "As a previous executive of a large company, I learned years ago the good that happens is not always passed to those who need to hear it most." I told him that I thought he should be aware of the hard work of UHD professors, how incredible Dr. Robertson and Dr. Gulati are and I explained the impact they were having on me in my first semester back. I let him know with all the I'S and ME's I could muster, how unfounded the original article by "Mr. Smith," was.

I received an email from Dr. Gulati during the holiday break in which she wrote, "David, even though your article was not selected for Dateline, I wanted you to know it is being read in high places." Later, I learned that Dr. Flores had placed my article in the right hands and the provost had passed it to the deans and someone in her department had commented about it. Net result, I was right, she is great and management at UHD acted on it in a positive way. Great organizations do things like that consistently as they pass on good things that happen and they share success as if it were their own. The life lesson here is that when you highlight the positive, when you complement people genuinely, when you follow the golden rule, it usually always comes back to you.

Subsequently, I learned that when UHD was deciding on nine students out of 14,000 for an advertising campaign, Dr. Gulati suggested that I was someone who represented students taking full advantage of the major opportunities at UHD. During the holidays, Diane Summers, a marketing executive at UHD contacted me via email. She said she too had read the article and that she was glad I had spoken up to express my personal feelings. She indicated that she would like me to consider being one of the nine featured students promoting UHD student success in an advertising campaign entitled, "Major Opportunity." I typed yes, hit send, and I high-fived the cat and the rest is literally the title of a book. The doors that have opened since then have been wide open and they speak volumes to an ongoing commitment by UHD administration and faculty to celebrate students as they pursue their opportunities in life.

I began this chapter by sharing an experience of attending a breakfast at the Houston Junior League honoring us as students. The opportunity presented to me by walking confidently through one open door at the University of Houston-Downtown is amazing. I suspect by now that you are in a better position to understand why the breakfast was special for all six of the UHD students in attendance. It was recognition for what can transpire when you look for, find and walk through a wide open door. I trust this book will illustrate that this concept is not exclusive to the doors of success accessible in all aspects of your life, including both your personal life and in business. The fact that this university recognizes, utilizes and rewards student involvement while publicizing their successes along the way as a top priority, sets them apart from any university that I know.

As I had already written much of the book prior to attending this event, I decided it was relevant to begin with this chapter and go in reverse. My goal is to share my business experiences and successes with you as a positive personal message and as a testimony that anyone can accomplish what they put their mind to at any age. I encourage each of you to accomplish what you can with the talent you possess. You can go back to school, you can earn a degree, you too can do what makes you happy and you too can apply your unique passion to accomplish your life work with pride. I am hopeful that as the result of reading my book you will be in a better position to focus on finding and opening your doors of major opportunity and are better prepared to knock on doors until you get inside. Any student, any employee, any parent, any member of management, any executive, for that matter, any person who has a desire to succeed, can do so. The principles of desire, attitude, persistence, effort and enthusiasm can overcome any obstacle that might block entrance to a door.

~ Chapter 2 ~
"One Door Leads to Another"

As a senior vice president of Stage Stores from 2000 through 2007, I was responsible for over $450 million in annual sales and 3,500 employees. Therefore, I served a seemingly important role in the company. From time to time, what arises due to that level of responsibility can be startling, even overpowering. The doors of opportunity would be many and I found over those years that repeatedly, one door would lead to another. During that seven-year period, I was on the company plane not once, but twice when the odds of survival would not be high under most any circumstances and gratefully, I survived both plane mishaps without a scratch. I begin chapter two with this story because in my ride to the top, it offers proof of the existence of a master plan and it validates the need to understand the importance of seizing opportunities each day of one's life. It demands a recognition that life is precious and serves as a constant reminder for me that one must learn to take advantage of open doors, especially when facing danger.

The first plane incident dramatically changed the corporate policy in our publicly held company headquartered in Houston. On the plane that day were our CEO, Jim Scarborough; my boss Ernie Cruse, the senior executive vice president—director of stores; Pat Bowman and myself, Sr. V.P.—equally responsible for

"Major Opportunities"

500 stores; the senior vice president of real estate; and the vice president of loss prevention. We were en route to visit a new store in one of my districts in Ennis, Texas for a grand opening celebration. We were on a propeller plane and all went well until we touched down, apparently hitting the only crack in the runway causing the landing gear to disengage and go back up into the plane. This is not a good thing as it results in a plane at 300 – plus miles per hour slowed to a stop by the literal grinding of the propellers into the ground on a short runway, without the landing gear in place. When we finally came to a stop, tilted downward, the plane was smoking profusely, with lubricants pouring out, now sitting stranded on the runway in a badly mangled private plane. Our lives flashed before our eyes and looking back, I must say that one has never seen a group of executives exit a plane so very quickly. It happened in slow motion as these things always do. As we bolted from the aircraft, with a fire engine and three of our district managers driving towards the wreckage, we could see we were lucky to be alive. The propellers were ground off the plane.

I must interject a lighter side of the story, one that speaks to how cool-headed and quick-witted my boss Ernie is. One of his jobs as a senior executive was to oversee all operations of the company plane. As part of that duty, it was his responsibility to complete an annual review of our pilot, Brian Bury. Once we were off the plane, realizing we were safe, Ernie turned to Brian our lifesaving pilot and calmly stated, "Heh Brian, you just had your annual review, it is a rating of very good and you will get a raise this year." We had a quick laugh from that moment of levity and it provides testimony to Ernie's uncanny ability to make the most of a bad situation. As we made phone calls to those we love, we continued to appreciate how blessed we were. Someone had a plan that day; a master plan for all of us, as there is for you as well. We avoided a door of disaster and were now heading through a different door altogether, called the future.

The airport administration officials in Ennis resurfaced that landing strip soon after our near disaster. Unfortunately, our plane was out of commission for many months after the incident. I had already been booked on a Southwest Airlines flight to return home as I was battling a horrible cold. The other passengers would spend the night in Dallas, some of them I suspect drinking down some leftover anxiety, perhaps with a buoyant smile knowing that we were granted another day of life. Instead, I went to Love Field and boarded another plane. I usually do not talk to people I am next to on planes but this time as I sat between two women, I simply could not resist saying to them, "Ladies, you would not believe what happened to me on the way to the airport." As I relayed the story of the crash, I am quite sure I scared the crap out of them because I watched as one began to pray silently for personal safety on this flight, grasping her crucifix and the other woman appeared to pop a Xanax or two.

I arrived home safely that evening and on Sunday morning when it was my usual time to offer the welcome, with a raspy voice from a lingering cold, I looked at the congregation and pointed out how blessed we are to have one more day to enjoy. I reminded them not to take anything in life for granted, not even for one day. The rest of the story from the company standpoint is relatively simple. Our board of directors quickly drafted a new corporate policy that prohibited certain individuals from being on the plane at the same time, which was a policy in a public company that was probably long overdue.

Now as if one crash is not enough, there was indeed a second one. As luck might have it, I was on the plane again with my boss Ernie and a couple of others I do not remember but I bet they remember it pretty well. This time as we landed we slid off the runway into the edge of a field. Although there were no propellers grinding into the ground, no fuel escaping, and no smoke billowing, Ernie, the wise man from the East, knew immediately there was another problem. His exact comment was, "That's not good." Brian our lifesaving pilot said, "We need to get off right now," which, of course, we did. We were actually well rehearsed at this procedure since we had practiced it once before in Ennis, Texas in crash number one.

"Major Opportunities"

This time though as we exited the plane, as Brian began to come down the ramp, he had to sit down. He was overcome, more so than he was in the first ordeal. As it turns out, we had problems with one of the engines as we landed requiring Brian to make a split second decision to land hot with one good engine throttled open and then as he hit a short runway, he had to stop on a dime. As it turns out, ninety-nine percent of the time this malfunction in a small propeller plane results in catastrophic loss of the plane as it typically causes a private plane to launch into a spiral at 300 miles per hour. It is the kind of scenario that you train for a lifetime to deal with in a second, hoping it never happens, not even once.

Just as I had felt after the first crash, the incident with the second plane malfunction was proof to me there was a master plan, especially for me, Brian and Ernie. What we accepted based upon what Brian explained was that we were lucky to be alive. I called my wife for a second time to tell her of the ordeal. I informed her that it had happened again, that we had experienced another major airplane malfunction and this time, we should be dead. She paused and then my usually even-keeled wife said, "That's it, I've had it." Fully expecting her to say, "There's no more flying on the private plane for you," I recall her response being something along the lines of, "That's it; I am raising your life insurance policy." Perhaps I have embellished her response ever so slightly—after all, it has been a while—but it does make for a humorous anecdote as presented.

No one can argue with any real persuasion that this was just good luck or a bad circumstance. Once? Maybe. Twice? No way! Some sort of grand plan twice provided rescue from the jaws of death for Ernie and me and the plan had Brian Bury in common both times. We still had things to do, people to see, places to go, and the door that remained open once again would lead to many new doors of opportunity for all of us. I am so grateful to Brian—not only is he a first rate pilot, but he is also an honest, decent, and trustworthy man. Thanks again Brian, you are a lifesaver.

As you are reading along, perhaps after you have a moment to reflect upon the story, I suspect you too can think of times in your life that provide an example of dramatic events that provide a stark reminder that life's opportunities are not to be taken for granted. You too may have had a close encounter helping you understand that one door may lead to another. My hope in sharing this true story with you is that it may shed light upon the value of second chances, upon doors of opportunities that remain open by taking life one day at a time. It is logical that at some point in one's life almost everyone has to wonder to them-selves what the plan for their future may be. Life certainly offers forks in the road and simple everyday decisions along the way can have a huge impact upon our lives.

Several more times over the years, incidents happened providing verification that a plan does exist in my life, occasionally, seemingly demanding divine intervention of sorts and this chapter provides testament of that. I believe we survived those plane incidents for a specific purpose. Four years ago, well after I had after I resigned from Stage Stores, Inc. I was driving toward Clear Lake to see my brother Steve at the car dealership where he works. It was rush hour traffic around 4 p.m. on the Gulf Freeway and I had my roof down as I was enjoying the beautiful weather and looking forward to seeing Stevie. I was in the far right lane when all of a sudden like a flash of light the driver in the middle lane lost complete control of her vehicle as she flipped twice, ending upside-down in her car with the roof completely smashed in. As the speeding flow of traffic halted to a complete stop, seeking to avoid becoming part of the wreckage, my car ended up directly across from hers with her body still trapped in the upside down vehicle. With the smell of gasoline, out of instinct, both I and another man, without hesitation, headed towards the spiraling car in an effort to help as we could.

As I think back to that day, I remember thinking the vehicle was going to explode at any moment as we rushed towards it with traffic bearing down on us. I did not know what condition we might find her in but without hesitation, we pulled a U.S. postal carrier out of her vehicle with tires still spinning and we quickly shuffled her to another car. The look on her face resembled one of confusion, horror, desperation and shock but there was not a scratch on her. The other cars in traffic were ready to go on by as I was trying to get back across the highway to re-enter my vehicle. I thought to myself ironically, "I had just pulled her out of her crushed vehicle and all these people wanted to do was to get on down the road." I exited the freeway and made a U-turn back to my brother's dealership. I walked in the front door and speaking to a stranger I stated, "You would not believe what just happened." As I explained the scary ordeal I had experienced, she made the comment, "Wow, you just saved her life." Still too shaken to respond, I thought, "No, God saved her, he has a plan for all of us, even her, and he had one for me to be there that day."

I suspect there are many other stories of circumstance, bravery, and survival to share but I know the fact I did not lose my life in either of those two plane mishaps was part of a master plan for me. It was a plan to be available that day, a plan requiring me to jump in when needed and to do what any decent man or woman would do. The plan for her that day was to keep going in life with a newly discovered perspective, perhaps trying to do more with her major opportunities in life.

So, let me ask you, is there a master plan for you? Have you seen, heard of, or perhaps even ignored things that have happened to you over the years that cause you to wonder? How do you know what the plan for you is? How do you execute a plan that you do not even understand exists? Have you ever stopped to think about it? The simple answer is yes; there is a plan for you and me. It is behind door number one or door number two, maybe even door number three, but it is there all right—you just have to begin looking for it.

Perhaps the real answers do not come as easily as I might suggest but there are some answers. As we begin our journey to explore how to maximize our potential I encourage you to make a commitment that no matter what you too will make an effort to enjoy and embrace every single day of your life, beginning today. Those two plane incidents changed my life but I hope you do not have to wait until you face a plane wreck, a car accident, or some personal tragedy before you consider your master plan and your role in life. I trust that this story and this book will offer encouragement as you consider things that happen along the way. Although it is a cliché to suggest that you do not know what tomorrow might bring, it is an accurate analogy and it offers proof that one door may lead to another!

If there is a master plan, how do we find it?

~ Chapter 3 ~
"All you have to do is Ask"

Maximizing a competitive nature developed through participation in sports and debate, I became one of the top sales men in the Bealls department store chain because I mastered the art of asking for what you want early on, and very persuasively. For the purposes of this chapter, "asking," means, knocking on the door of success. This essential sales tool of asking is often the distinction between achieving great sales results and accepting average results in most professions. It is often the difference between constantly making your sales numbers and consistently missing your numbers. As frustrating as it is to deal with a constant stream of no's, there is a blueprint one can follow that can result in a higher percent of yes responses. Asking for a yes by knocking, must be practiced consistently and relentlessly on your path of moving through the doors of yes.

It's simple, but it's redundant. It's simple, but it's monotonous. It's simple, but it's exhausting. You have to be willing to ask repeatedly, and then you have to ask again, one more time. Then, you have to ask differently, one more time. You cannot stop asking; you can never stop knocking on the door. The one person you do not ask is the one who would have said yes. In addition, the one door that you do not knock on will stay closed. Everyone tells you that asking for what you want is a good plan but most do not explain to you, train you, or help you become comfortable fending off those no's, thereby increasing the number of yeses you get and as a result, building your confidence.

No is not a fun word to hear. No one likes to get no for an answer so in certain cases they simply just stop asking, and they take the easy way out. One may miss the opportunity door altogether by assuming they will not get a yes or that they will definitely get a no—both are true if you think about it. Not asking, not even knocking at the door is a no. Retail 101 for anyone in sales is never stop trying because when you stop trying you tend to lose most of the time.

However, how do top sales employees in any profession get to the top? They learn to ask more persuasively; they master the art of asking. The best of the best in sales will explain that the odds of getting a no are directly proportional to the number of times you ask the question. The challenge for most sales representatives is that they either hate rejection (as most people do), they do not know how to ask, or they do not know how to ask in a way that gets a yes often enough. As a result, they are tempted at some point to stop asking or to quit. Unfortunately, all three of the obstacles can interfere with even the best-intentioned, most enthusiastic employee. There are thousands of resources recommending how to do it but allow me to offer real-life examples that I know helped me get to the top of sales. They are the same ones that can help you on your way to the top as well.

I had to want to get a yes—a yes equals Success!

For this former competitive debater, getting a yes meant winning and everyone loves to win, don't they? When I made the choice to bypass the completion of my degree at HBU I understood I needed to go get a job. I chose to get married, and having a good job was an obligation as I proceeded into the world. All I knew was debate but debate was over. My fiancée actually landed my first real opportunity to knock at Bealls department Store in

"Major Opportunities"

Houston, a family-owned business headquartered in Jacksonville, Texas. A few years earlier Bealls purchased Battlesteins in Houston, which turned out to be only one of the imminent disasters the company would face down the road. My fiancée worked at a bank in Sharpstown Mall and she worked part-time at night behind the customer service desk at Bealls department store. Management must have thought well of her, because they granted me an interview. One knock and a door opened but my timing was terrible. I went in for my first interview in January when the majority of retailers cut their payrolls back to the bare bone so it was only one of those slightly open doors that you have to stick your head inside of that I mentioned earlier.

The first interview was a "No, but thanks for stopping by," stopping short of, "We do not need help right now," or, "We only took this interview because we like your girlfriend, but please check back and it was so nice to finally meet you." As a result, my future wife and I continued to enjoy fine dining at the local Burger King, and a few weeks later, I checked back a second time, this time deciding to get straight to the store manager Bob Hart. My fiancée had shared how wonderful he was and I figured, why not go to the top this time to ask. I decided to knock on a bigger door. Amazingly, he agreed to see me. I put on a suit and pulled together a resume consisting of a shoelace and a prayer on a single piece of paper that noted no degree but lots of debating success, and I carried a look in my eyes of genuine desire. I told him I needed a job, pure and simple, and that I believed I could apply the same competitive spirit I had used in debate to win for him, his store, and for his company. However, after thirty minutes of him telling me how great the company is, how much opportunity there was, he then told me payroll was tight in January, that I should be patient and come back again; in other words, my second no.

The dining continued for us at the local Burger King. To be honest with you, as I look back those were some of the most meaningful dates we had. It was not about fine dining; instead, it was about a love, a kindred friendship, a longing to be together, to dream together, and to keep our hopes alive. Three weeks later, I knocked for a third time on the door by calling the store and this time I left a message for the assistant manager to call me when he could. I said that I was "Just checking back." In a few days, I received the call I had been waiting on and I was hired and informed that I could start to work the following week. I had finally received my first yes. I just had to keep asking, keep knocking, more than once. All you have to do is knock and often asking is the loudest knock one can make.

The first question I asked when I stepped into my new sales position was probably the same as a typical person who desires to become successful quickly might ask. I said, "So how do you get to the top of this company, anyway?" A divisional manager informed me that you have to make the sales report consistently, meaning that you are one of the top twenty sales associates in the company in a given month. "Also, you learn how to merchandise several different departments in the store," he added. Therefore, over the next two years I obsessed on out-selling everyone in the chain and learning how to merchandise. The two are very different as they are two different doors altogether but I had to go through both of them in order to keep opening my doors of success.

Jumping forward in time, as a way to garner some credibility from you, in a retail clothing chain of 150 stores I would go on to break lots of sales records in the company. I would be number two in the company for total yearly sales in the shoe division, and in the men's department, I was number one on a regular basis on the monthly sales report, rarely falling below the top ten on any report for the two years I was competing on the sales floor. It was just like winning many debate rounds without having to carry all that heavy evidence around from building to building for days on end. I kept on knocking and the doors of yes kept on opening, the same doors I want you to knock on too.

In the end, all I had to do was to ask for what I wanted—a job, then I had to ask what to do to be successful at it, and then I just had to go do it. You have to want it badly enough; you have to be hungry enough, motivated enough, and professional enough in pursuing your desire to be excellent, something you too can do in

"Major Opportunities"

any field you choose. Nothing has changed today—it still has 99% to do with your drive, your ambition, and your effort. Remember, I was not down on my luck as I was used to winning, I just needed to find a major opportunity and to keep knocking on more doors. When I make the statement, "All you have to do is ask," what I really mean is also a life lesson. You have to ask! And while most of the time, no one will turn you down if you don't ask, no one will say yes if you don't ask. Those who knock increase the chance of getting what they want in direct proportion to the number of times they ask. In doing so, they are able to open the same door that others avoid knocking on, simply by asking.

Let me provide an example of the most important opportunity door I knocked on. As it turns out the store manager, Mr. Bob Hart, contrary to popular opinion in upper management circles, actually hated being in Houston. As I found out later, he wanted out of the big city of Houston, Texas. He had served as a regional manager years before and had suffered some heart health issues and was now being effectively used by the company to run a high volume store in a tough competitive market.

Bob Hart finally got his wish in fall 1983 when he left to manage a new store in Tyler, Texas that swiftly became one of the best stores in the chain. Speaking of "Major Opportunities," he took my wife and me with him as he made me his senior manager trainee. It would turn out to be the Tyler store that would launch my climb to the top over the next sixteen years. It would be a climb to Senior V.P. of Stage Stores in 2000 where I would oversee 200 stores, 14 district managers, and 3,500 employees, all thanks to asking for a job that began with two no's and a yes! If I had not asked, I would not have gone with him and I have no clue what I would now be writing in this chapter. One door, one opportunity, can change a life, forever.

One significant fact in this story is that I had only heard a rumor that Mr. Hart was in the running for the Tyler position. After another date at Burger King and a discussion with my wife, I decided to corner him in the sign room as I blurted out excitedly, "So I heard you might be moving to Tyler, Mr. Hart, is Tyler a good place to raise a family?" From the corner of his eye, Santa Claus winked, smiled, and flew back up the chimney quickly saying, "So, Dave you and Karen might like Tyler, you think?" "Well let's just think about that," "Hmmm, you just never know what is ahead of you do you, Dave?" As I watched him ascend I replied, "Well, it might be nice to move away and start on our own." Christmas came early that year, as Mr. Hart decided to take us with him to East Texas and not even aware of it, I began my journey to the top of a tall mountain, one that I refer to as "Mount Success," the same mountain you too can begin to climb, right now.

All I had to do was ask, by knocking on another door!

Mr. Hart became a close friend over those next 15 years and as a mentor, he taught me much more than retail; he taught me how to make money, increase sales, improve profit, and how to seek balance in life. I loved him dearly and when he passed away from liver cancer years later, I missed a family ski trip the week after Christmas to attend his funeral. It was a tough trip traveling towards Tyler that day. I reflected upon how one single man had influenced others so positively and so permanently. I reflected how he never missed an opportunity over fifteen years in person or by phone, praising my successes as if they were his own, to encourage me to stay grounded, to give me the best advice he could and to stay in my life as a constant even during the sickness that was taking his life. Even when he came to Houston to seek treatment at the medical center, he found his way to my home with his lovely wife Anne, making it a point to share his love and affection with me and little did I know it would be the last time I would see him in this life. I miss him dearly and I still think about him in some way or another often.

During the course of completing this book, I found myself reaching out to his wife Anne. As we talked and then emailed each other over the course of a few weeks last holiday season, I somehow felt as though Mr. Hart's wise counsel was still there. I saw his smile and somehow I thought I could hear his encouraging voice telling me to be what I could be. Understanding it was her voice speaking on his behalf, I remembered what I had almost forgotten, that she too knew and loved the same Bob Hart I did, as they had been high school sweethearts. Do not be afraid to tell someone this very day what they mean to you.

Do you know a Bob Hart? I bet you do! There are Bob Harts out there, everywhere—you just have to listen, look and find one. I believe you too have at least one person watching and listening to you. Your success they see as theirs, your pain they see as painful, your joy they rejoice in silently and your success allows them to experience success. Bob Hart taught me all about creating the best customer service experience you can for your customer. It is because of Bob Hart that I developed a much clearer understanding of how customer service guarantees success. His management style was unique for, "He only did, what only he could do," which I will explain in a subsequent chapter on mentoring. He stayed on the floor a high percent of the time, his people skills were impeccable and he led by example. I applied from his management style some of those most important traits that made me the executive and leader I became.

Adapting some of Mr. Hart's style helped me develop my own management style, "Don't ask someone to do what you are not willing to do yourself." I did not have the benefit of Bob Hart's wisdom or experience at the time and I had to find the style that worked best for me as a young manager. Both of these theories of management could benefit leaders in all facets of the private and public sectors even today. Too often in retail it seems that due to a manager's lack of experience they rely upon, "Just do what I say." Relying upon this style to manage is a bad model to imitate and is ultimately doomed from the beginning. Leading by example is the best way to lead; showing them how to do it is better, teaching them versus just telling them is best. There are three other mentors in my career that I will discuss in another chapter but for now please accept that one person can change a life, one person can teach you how to lead and one person can transform another into being the best they can be.

Mainly, through persistence, I received a yes and opened a door wide open for the next 24 years. I know that as hungry as I was for those inexpensive Burger King dates, I had more of an appetite to prove that my skills as a former national circuit debater could translate to the real world as success. I knew I could win at most anything I competed at but what I needed to learn and then to master was how to apply management skills to motivate others to win—how to persuade others to enjoy winning with me. I wanted to prove to myself that all those years of carrying heavy debate cases from round to round could pay off. If I had not been persistent or if I had taken either of the first two no's, that door of opportunity might easily have closed.

Higher education, intelligence, training and development, people skills and even operational skills are important to success but sharing it with others distinguishes one as special. The persistence and desire with which you go after a yes and the strength of pursuit of your passion can result in your own successes simply by using your talents. Let me share some simple rules of engagement that can help guarantee a yes for you like it did for me so many times beginning with—

Always ask with a YES in mind!

As I reflect upon the importance of asking with a yes in mind, I recall a letter my daughter Kaitlyn wrote when she was 10 and the response I gave her. I have her permission to include this letter in the book as I have used the story several times over the past 10 years since it occurred. The only way to tell this story is to include both of the letters for you to read.

"Major Opportunities"

Katie and Dad

Kaitlyn's Letter

Dearest father whom I adore no matter what your answer is, I have two requests for you to consider. Please read them carefully and try to be open-minded as you consider my ideas. Mom said I needed to talk to you about them but I think I have her support — at least she did not say no. First, I think it is time for me to start wearing some make up. I will eventually wear make up on a daily basis and I think using an eye shadow and possibly some lipstick would help me practice for the future. Madison will eventually need to wear make-up (but not before me) and I could become her personal trainer. My friend Janie's mother already said yes, I am hoping you are as open-minded as she is. Second Daddy, I think it is time for me to start shaving my legs. Daddy, I know you may not know it but I am becoming hairy. Daddy, it is not good for a young girl to be so very hairy. I talked with mommy and she said that she completely understands my problem. Once again, Madison will need to shave someday soon and I could be her personal coach. Daddy, I know you are very busy but I need a response so I can get started. No matter what, I will love you despite whatever decision you decide to make. I hope it is a good one.

Signed, your loving, appreciative princess, Kaitlyn Alyssa Slaughter

PS. I would like a response within 48 hours

Daddy's Response

My dearest daughter Princess Kaitlyn, whom I too adore, I have read your letter carefully as you suggested and I have considered your requests including visiting with your mother about it and I have the following answers for you. First, in terms of the make-up request, I have three responses. No, absolutely – not and under no circumstance. Katie, you are still too young to begin wearing make-up in our opinion. You will have plenty of time in the future to use make-up. Please be patient, your time is coming. I do appreciate your offer to become a trainer for your sister though, she will be glad to know you are thinking about her when she is only eight. Second, in terms of the hairy leg situation, I feel your pain. For you see Katie, I too am hairy. I agree with your request to start shaving your legs, effective immediately. A word of caution, avoid the use of Nair at all costs. I tried it on my legs once when I was a young boy thinking it might help the hair on my legs grow. It burns a lot; avoid this burn at all costs. Instead, I recommend you consider a Lady Schick. I think they are pink, like a princess might use. Please be careful when you shave and remember Kaitlyn, the first cut is the deepest. By the way, under no circumstance may use my Braun razor on your legs, it is strictly forbidden. I love you with all my heart.

Signed, your open minded father, David Neill Slaughter

PS. I responded within 12 hours; please learn from that my little grasshopper.

"Major Opportunities"

In my fatherly opinion, a letter like that is worthy of major consideration by any parent as proper justification to buy this book. I suspect many of you have similar stories that might haunt your child well into your late years as it too becomes greatly exaggerated. In the meantime, it seems clear that Kaitlyn had asked, with a yes in mind. Although she never became a debater, I suspect she would have been a good one. She got one no and one yes by asking in a way that persuasively made me find a way to say yes at least once. By the way, as I am sure you Dads can relate to, since that time I have said yes many times and of course, she just keeps on asking. Yes responses are directly proportional to how you ask, how many times you ask it, and to what extent you prepare for the asking — and my Katie prepared very well for the asking!

Translated to my real world of retail, I accepted the task of writing and preparing a new charge solicitation manual for 10,000 employees at Stage Stores Inc. back in 2002-2003, a handbook presented to new hires as part of their training process. The title I picked for the handbook was, "All You Have to do is Ask." The opening of charge accounts contributed up to thirty-five percent of our annual company sales and is still important to my ex-company and to other large box retailers today. The energy and excitement generated because of the knowledge shared in that employee handbook was critical as a way to inspire our employees to open charge accounts on a daily basis, the same charge accounts so very vital to a consistent return business in our stores. In the end, it was still just as simple as asking for it, just another door to open.

The more sales employees asked, the more new charge accounts we opened. The more they opened, the more money they made. The more they opened, the more their effective hourly rate became, with no limit placed as to how much they could improve their earnings. The more accounts we all opened, the more return business the company had each year. The slogan that became our battle cry remained, "All you have to do is ask!" Stores that did not ask did not usually achieve their sales goals. Stores that were not asking usually had sales results below the district or company average.

Realistically, too many of the times employees asked the answer was no, so getting a yes meant they must ask a second or third time. Whether it be opening new accounts, closing a simple sale, getting a customer to trade up to a more expensive item, or simply making a sales pitch, it is not as easy as it sounds in theory—, which presents a Major Opportunity. Too often in the retail sales world I have witnessed people who rely upon the same sales pitch over and over again hoping the answer will be yes the next time around. I have heard it repeated that the definition of insanity is doing the same thing repeatedly and expecting a different result, and that is actually true when it comes to turning a no into a yes in sales.

It takes at least two no's to get a Yes!

One mistake sales folks make is stopping with only one no. It takes at least two no's before one is getting a real no. If you are getting no's consistently, you have to consider changing your pitch, or your message, perhaps even your method of presentation. This means asking for and receiving feedback from people who are consistently successful and mimicking their behavior until it becomes your own. One of the best employees I have watched master the art of asking was in Corpus Christi, Texas, her name is Dalia Perez. My store was over 50,000 square feet and did almost $10 million in annual sales with tons of foot traffic every single day of the year. Dalia opened about 130 new accounts each month, bringing in another $8-$10 per hour just by securing new charge accounts for that Bealls department store.

There are many ways to overcome objections!

I observed the "Dalia Perez" method of disabling objections one day from afar. Dalia dressed like a million dollars to begin with, which always helps open the first door and when she greeted

"Major Opportunities"

a customer she would usually always compliment them on what they were wearing, drawing them into a conversation. She would quickly make her first pitch by saying, "I bet you already have one of our charge cards, don't you, sweetheart?" When they said yes she would say, "Exactly, well let's go spend some money." When they said no she would say, "Exactly, well it's time to change that so you can get all of our discounts." I watched the customer that particular day as she applied the most challenging objection, the dreaded, "My husband would kill me" response. The customer went on to say, "He just gripes about charge accounts, he . . . he . . . he just doesn't understand the benefits, I have tried to tell him." Dalia listened very patiently and then said to her without even batting an eye, "Exactly, we'll let me show you how to do it, sweetheart!" Like a lamb to the slaughter, the customer walked with Dalia to the register and began to fill out the short application for credit as if she was now seemingly in a deep trance of some sort.

Often the best way to overcome an objection is to make it seem like the most unimportant decision of the day. I watched as Dalia sold her $1,000 worth of new merchandise and as she was leaving Dalia said to the woman, "Now why don't you go buy your husband a little gift with that $100 you just saved. I bet he's not gonna kill you after all, now will he?" The woman smiled and I thought to myself, "Cha-ching." The objection was over-come, we had another happy customer and we were guarantee future business. With my observation of a perfect formula, I just kept looking for and hiring more Dalia's and my business kept on growing from year to year.

Recently, I decided to call and talk to Dalia in Corpus one evening. I could not resist as my curiosity was getting the best of me. I took the liberty of calling her after 10 long years to thank her for what she taught me and for being a "Top Gun and my leader." As I suspected, she is still on the sales floor in Corpus Christi, Texas, still giving GREAT customer service, still opening charge accounts, still talking about how easy it is do it with me on the phone. Some things just never change—once a "Top Gun," always a "Top Gun," and getting a yes has a lot to do with asking a second time or a third time and by asking the right way every time.

Learning to minimize objections is critical to success!

Objections to what you are asking one to do seem to be one of the biggest obstacles prohibiting closing the highest percent of sales. Years ago, when writing that charge solicitation handbook I mentioned, the most important instructions centered upon making sure they were prepared to answer objections by minimizing the significance of the decision. For example, when a customer would object by saying they had too many credit cards, the natural response would be to say, "Well then one more won't matter and you can save 10% on your sale today." That would amount to $X, Mrs. Brown. Or if someone said, "The interest rate is too high on credit cards" the natural response would be, "Well if you pay it off each month there is no interest charge but you still get the mailers and special discounts we offer you through the mail." Occasionally, a customer would use the dreaded, "My husband will kill me response," the one that I watched Dalia fight off that one day. Although it can be a difficult objection to overcome, truthfully, it is just one more excuse and you deal with it head on. However, I have never read on the internet, "HUSBAND MURDERS WIFE BECAUSE OF ONE MORE CREDIT CARD!" An objection is just that, it is a reason to say no to you. Training, knowledge, skill, and a positive attitude are all proven ways to overcome most of the objections one might encounter.

Overcoming objections is not as difficult as one might make it. You cannot simply throw out the asking and then accept no as a final answer without giving them a good reason to reconsider their quick decision. The example I use in this chapter applies to opening credit card accounts but it also applies to other forms of suggestive selling, and in general, it applies to how you sell yourself. You have to give them a tangible, compelling, reasonable justification to say yes or to change their mind from no. You must make an effort to address their objections head on. People are surprisingly decent and open-minded much of the time, I have discovered.

Something I learned early on and that I did not forget is that in most retail, you never know what circumstance the customer is escaping. There is usually a good reason they are out fighting the crowds in the malls. They either want something, they want to get away from someone, they want to spend someone else's money, they are bored, they are unhappy, they seek that special feeling you get when you treat yourself to what you deserve. Perhaps they are escaping any number of things driving them crazy, including a significant other, boyfriend, girlfriend or spouse. Typically, they want to buy something for themselves and that caveat applies to every single retailer I am aware of, to just about every kind of business. Assume they will buy and that they are there because they want something. Assume they need cheering up by being convinced to purchase something for one of their most favorite people, themselves. Most of the time you just have to ask and be willing and capable to meet an objection head on with a confident, consistently applied, truthful answer and a big smile.

In retail, for that matter when it comes to the purchase of a home, cars, electronics, even purchases in grocery stores, the assumption that customers are just looking, is a false assumption. "I am just looking," is not a no; it is not really even an objection. It is most likely a canned programmed response to stall you, to distract you or to suggest to you to, "Leave me alone, you vulture of pressure — you giant praying mantis." I expected my employees to ask if they could help customers as a consistent way to speak to them, to open the conversation but more importantly to look for a door of opportunity that might allow them to maximize what we were there to do, to sell something and to provide great service. You can assume they are just looking but you must focus on helping them turn "just looking," into a desire, into making a transition to buy. Whether it is clothing, electronics, soft goods, hard goods, homes or cars, they are there because they want to buy something, usually for themselves. You know it, they know it, we all know it, so stop saying "May I help you," and open the door wide open by complimenting them, identifying what they are looking for, by making them feel important and by simply talking one on one with them and smiling.

Too much pressure you ask, no, not really. Buyer's remorse does happen—we know that, especially with big-ticket items but rarely in my twenty-four years of sales can I remember someone walking in, throwing items on the wrap stand and defiantly saying, "I have had it with myself, I deserve nothing, nothing at all, in fact I am no longer speaking to myself!" It may be the one occupying their nest at home or perhaps inside their head still talking to them, it may be the one they are escaping from in the first place as they go shopping. It is somewhat ironic, isn't it, but often very true?

Saying please and thank you—still matters!

You might assume the average person has mastered a simple extension of courtesies early in life, but not so. I have observed repeatedly over the years that common courtesy, genuineness, and sincerity add significantly to excellence in sales results, yet it is often lacking in consistency. As old school as it may be, thanking people every single time for a sale by name, looking them in the eye, giving them a handshake, or a smile at the end regardless of the size of a sale is important to gaining repeat customers. Many of the most successful sales people I know still take the time to send thank you notes, birthday cards and reminders as a professional way to stay in touch and are still a simple personal way to stay in someone's mind on a regular basis.

On the other hand, in my opinion, there is too much emphasis placed on the use of business cards. I know, business cards are essential to networking, recruiting, and extending business opportunities; therefore, they are indeed important. How they look, the paper they are on, and the design is relevant to the statement you and your company want to make as a "brand," but what is most important is the one-on-one personal experience someone has with you, as it can instill a lasting memory. The business card is just simply a record of that memory. The number of business cards printed and given out is not a great measurement for future success. Instead, I would argue it is a special ability, the opportunity to create a one-on-one personal experience as a way to obtain a long-term business relationship.

Learn to celebrate yes and forget about the no's

Celebrating yes is important but learning to forget the no's is more important. Management must train their staff to remain engaged in the trenches with their heads up, fighting off negative while feeding off positive. Learning to celebrate yes by watching, listening, and seeing what your employees do right is a great way to make the no's they receive seem more palatable, seem like they're just a part of the job. We may forget that our employees are the ones in the trenches with their little battle helmets on sticking their heads up to say, "Could you buy this customer, please?" The part we forget is that it is not fun to hear no often and this rejection makes our employees numb with failure. Unless they are re-charged or re-motivated through extra incentive or reward, they may stop asking altogether.

Financial rewards are awesome, but I have found that most often consistent praise and recognition is the most effective long-term motivational tool to get them to continue to do what is part of their job. As a team leader, no matter what challenge you are presenting to an employee, you will obtain the best results if you get out on the playing field with them. You are better off if they see you are willing to go out on the battlefield with them with your little helmet on as it is empowering to them and the respect you earn will pay huge dividends in your own career advancement down the road. I have determined over years in retail that there is not enough celebration of the yeses obtained along the way. Getting excited over small successes paves the road to celebrate the bigger ones as the ones to remember. It is so much easier to block out the failures of no's by celebrating a yes. Do not dwell on failures; dwell upon wins and victories often.

One has to keep swinging at every single pitch!

My favorite personal sales success stories is one I want to share because it speaks to the fact that one miss, one time of not asking, can deny landing the biggest fish in the lake. In accordance with what I am instructing you to do, I never stopped swinging at pitches. When I was on the sales floor in Tyler in 1985, I experienced another top-of-the-mountain major sales opportunity. Interestingly, it occurred as we were closing the store late one Saturday night. The procedure at the end of our day was to close out the register, preparing a till for the morning opening staff. It was right at our nine p.m. closing time after a very busy retail Saturday, and I was exhausted. I looked up and out of the corner of my eye, I saw a man and a woman browsing inexpensive Hagar suits on the back wall of the men's department. I recognized that no one else was paying attention, therefore, this time I would not have to race to beat someone to the customer. I closed my register drawer quickly and I walked briskly towards them as if it was my first sale of the day and as if rest was not on my agenda.

As it turns out, he was the vice president of a local bank out shopping after dinner with his girlfriend, who mentioned she had been nagging him to come in for his usual "once a year," shopping trip. I liked the tone of "Once a year." He added, "Well they need to close sweetie, we will just come back some other time." My response was, "No Sir, we are open until you are finished and we are not leaving until your yearly shopping trip is complete." He looked at me; she nodded to him as if to say, "If you do not do this, I will not let you forget it." Long story short, we left at 11:45 pm that Saturday night with the air conditioning shutting down automatically long before that late hour. Our assistant manager,

"Major Opportunities"

Mike Mayfield called in the final sales number to Bob Hart every night and he finally gave him a courtesy call saying, "David has a very big fish on the line and it appears he is reeling him in slowly but it's a big one and it's stuck on the line." Mr. Mayfield added that he thought we were going to have a much better sales increase than he had previously thought based upon huge stacks of merchandise I kept gleefully adding to a pile at the register.

When the banker and his girlfriend left that evening, he had purchased 6 suits, 12 dress shirts, 15 ties, six pairs of shoes, 18 pairs of socks, lots of undershirts and underwear, three belts, six pairs of dress slacks, three sport coats, six casual slacks, six casual sport shirts, and a partridge in pear tree! The sale was right at $4,500 and back in 1984 that was like hitting $12,000 these days in one sale. As I lay exhausted on the sales floor, Bob Hart had indeed waited to go to sleep until he received the final number—not out of greed, but out of excitement. In the end, the store had improved for the day by another 10 percent and I ended with $8,000 for the day in total sales. That one sale ended my fiscal month both on commission and on the company monthly sales report, with a huge bang. That one sale permitted me to be number one in the entire chain of 156 stores by $1,800.00 for the very first time. This story was one I knew back then, as I smiled a sigh of exhausted relief, I would keep in the back of my mind. It would be one I was sure that over the years would allow me to make this point to someone, for you. It offers a lesson that one cannot stop swinging at pitches and that sometimes the best hits may come at a time when you least expect them, but perhaps when you need them the most. You simply cannot overlook any customer no matter how late they walk in, no matter how they dress and no matter how tired you are.

Since we have been exploring the odds of obtaining a positive response, it is noteworthy that baseball players provide one of the best analogies demonstrating a need to keep swinging at the pitch until you hit one it out of the park. To illustrate, a great baseball player, Babe Ruth, comes to mind. I suspect many of us have heard of the Babe as being one of the greatest baseball players of all time. For years, he held the record for the most home runs over the course of professional baseball history, among many others. Most baseball enthusiasts, if asked, would recognize him as one of if not the best home run hitter of all time but. Guess who holds the record for striking out the most as well? You got it, Babe Ruth! Having shared that fact do you think that when the Babe came up to bat, even if he had struck out the first time or even the second time at bat in a game that the fans thought he was going to strike out? Of course not! When he stepped up to home plate, they would say, "Watch this, the Babe is gonna hit it out of the park again, I bet you he does, right now, I betcha!" That's because everyone knew that the Babe just kept on swinging for the fences and he kept on hitting it out of the park. Babe Ruth once responded when asked about striking out three times in one game, "Never let the fear of striking out get in your way."

The Babe was right and he understood that every sales person, every sales manager, anyone who desires to be number one, must understand that the fear of striking out, that a fear of getting a no, that the fear of rejection; has no place in winning. Winners keep swinging. We just need to become little Babe Ruth's as we keep swinging at the pitch until we knock one out of the park. In the game of baseball, in the game of sales, in the game of life, "All you have to do is ask," and consistency in results means you are consistently knocking on the "Major Opportunities" doors of success, so start knocking!

But which door is the right one for me?

~ Chapter 4 ~
"Opening the Right Door"

As self-serving as it might appear, I could not write this book about "Major Opportunities" without giving you some of the "Toot your own horn" story, as a model for what any over-achiever can accomplish. Actually, I am proud of the successes I enjoyed over those twenty-four years in retail clothing sales in spite of not having received my degree, until now, of course. Accomplished with help from others, it was also due to a strong drive and passion on my part as well. My success was generated by a combination of factors including: learning from the best as mentors; learning from my own mistakes; applying God-given talent and translating it to skill; and as a result of surrounding myself with the best people and creating an atmosphere in which they could flourish. It was a result of opening the right door and by making the right decision about which door to enter next.

In my case, as is true in most cases representing a rise from sales that open a door to enter management, requires a high level of sales success. After that, as one drives to the top of an organization or company, it requires an acceptance that you generally move up due to people who help you succeed, not just your results. If you ever stop believing that, if you remove yourself from the simple reality that you put your pants on just as the next person does, you run a high risk of a fall from grace. From the second you walk through that first door of opportunity called management, the opportunity to succeed and to win through others, begins.

I never asked them to do what I was not willing to do!

I definitely worked hard for twenty-four years but I did it with great people at my side. I say at my side because I never asked them to do what I was not willing to do. Let me say that again, "I never asked them to do what I was not willing to do!" Warned repeatedly over the years that I would burn out I heard, "Wonder boy, you better be careful, you are going to lose your hair someday," or "You better be careful, you don't want to die young,?" or "You're going to have a heart attack someday, slow down boy. I also heard them say, "You don't want an ulcer, do you?" I often thought to myself when they said something like that it had more to do with their own insecurity or a lack of desire. I could see it in their silent, gossiping, jealous eyes that they did not get it, they probably do not get it now, and they will probably never get it. I might be willing to say now "No, I am going to be the best I can be, the very best I can be. I am going to stay out on the sales floor, let my employees see me as the example I know I need to be." In retrospect, I might have added, "By the way, I am going to lead them to the top of a mountain and we are going to stay there for as long as we can." Now, I might even have the courage to say, "By the way, I am 55 and do I look like I lost any hair?" Honestly, I would probably still just let the results do the talking—that was always the best way anyway; that will usually always shut them up.

Translated from my seemingly sarcastic tone back to reality, what I would mean in my silent responses to myself is that, "I will lead them, I will pull them, I will push them, but mostly, I will show them we are better, that we can be the best, that we will do our best no matter what. I will reassure them that we are stars, each and every one, and that together as a team of stars we cannot and will not be beat, and that we are unique enough, good enough and proud enough to get there and to stay there, despite obstacles, disappointments, and defeat."

I say to you my readers, that when you do get to the top of that mountain of success with a team you build and work side by side with, look out among the valleys and cities below with a strong sense of satisfaction because you did it together. Typically, they like the air up there, they tend to want to stay on top, and you are able to keep them high on that mountain of success for a long time with a special sense of pride being the best they can be every single day. It is all about having a fun, exciting, dynamic work place where people want to go, and it feels great.

That first major opportunity door had been the one my wife opened for me in Bealls department store in Houston. Do you remember? It was the same job I had asked Bob Hart to give me, the door that I had to knock on three times to get someone to open wide. Well that one door opened the first big door that would lead me on a path to the top of a great company years later. I had definitely opened the right door, but I must tell you in retrospect that I almost went through the wrong door. I have to tell you all about that experience hoping perhaps you can avoid my mistakes. After obtaining that first yes in the Houston Bealls store, I began receiving something like nine to fifteen hours a week. Remember, I landed that job in the slowest time of the year and therefore, understandably, the Burger King meals continued for us. I was now waiting my turn for a manager trainee position to become available and no one really knew when that would be. They kept telling me to sell as much as I could every single day, that my time would come. In the meantime, with as little patience as I had and being hungry for more than a Burger King hamburger, I took a big uncalculated risk.

I had heard through the grapevine that the previous assistant manager of my current store was on the lookout for a manager trainee for his new store. Reluctantly, I decided to go visit his store on a day off to inquire about the position, without telling Mr. Hart that I was interested. I interviewed with the store manager and with the assistant and they could see I was eager for an opportunity to get into a management position. I mentioned I was interested in advancement but I told them I was not exactly sure how to broach the topic with my store manager, Mr. Hart. As I spoke, I sensed my risk was growing. The store manager, sensing my uncomfortable predicament, suggested that he might just casually mention it in polite conversation with Mr. Hart, perhaps when they spoke next. He indicated he would simply say he had heard I was interested. I headed back to my store the next day feeling slightly guilty for thoughts of mutiny against the kind man that had provided my first major opportunity, the man who had opened the first door. As the next few days passed, I reflected upon how premature I had been to place myself in a situation like that. There was now a real possibility that I would not even like the smaller volume store as it was much farther away from home and I actually loved where I was working already. Finally, I had some slight fear of how Mr. Hart might feel about this coup (coup d'état) I was now part of. That Saturday I was working in the children's department and I saw Mr. Hart out of the corner of my eye as he was heading out of the store for the day. My eyes betrayed me by looking in his direction. As they did, he said the following to me as he smiled from ear to ear, "Dave, you didn't really think I was going to let you get away from me, did you?" With a blank stare on my face, sensing that there was nothing to say in return that made sense, I said to him, "No sir, I love it here, I love working for you." He smiled and as he walked out, I realized how much I loved that man. Two weeks later, promoted to manager trainee, he shook my hand and he said, "Dave, I am glad you chose to stay with us." Sometimes a door closes and another door opens. Finding the right door is important as you become actively involved in your master plan. Choose wisely, think it through, and focus upon what door of opportunity you want to walk through.

As we explore doors that open in life, it is important we remember that it is up to us to decide which ones to knock on and which ones to walk through. Most assuredly, if I had entered that other door, leaving Mr. Hart for the smaller store—my life, my results, everything would have been different. By the way, the other store closed later as did all of the Bealls stores in Houston and that door might easily have been the one that closed my door of success at Stage Stores Inc. Fortunately, I chose the right door when I knocked those three times, and in turn, Mr. Hart opened the door wide for me. I encourage you to look closely at your doors of opportunity paying close attention to the size of the door, and to who is behind the door standing.

Sometimes, YOU just have to say NO!

This story, written in the final stages of editing the book; at the very point in time, I was faced with a need to cut a chapter or to reduce the book by 8,000 words. This was necessary in order to meet the specifications I had agreed to, serving the interest of everyone in the project, so naturally, I wrote more. I could not exclude this next story as it provides proof that sometimes you have to look ahead to the long-term picture and sometimes, you have to have the courage to say no. I decided to hunt down one of the best management people I ever had report to me. Her name is Monica Smiley. It comes as no surprise to me she is doing well in Florida as a Regional Marketing Manager at Villas of Grand Cypress with Benchmark Hospitality.

Although I spent a lot of time in this chapter helping you overcome no, providing advice on how to be successful by dealing with, avoiding and getting around the no's in life, sometimes, when it comes to you, to your own career, you just have to say no. Monica is also in another chapter and at the risk of tooting my own horn again, here is what she wrote on the professional social networking site, LinkedIn, "Thanks for always reinforcing the philosophy that you do what's right not what's easy. I learned so much from you, and compare every working relationship I have ever had to you . . . and I have not found anyone that meets your standards yet."

David Slaughter

As we visited between Pensacola, Florida and Houston for an hour, we shared many stories that provide memories of a lifetime. One of those stories relevant to this chapter is a reminder she provided pertaining to the day the earth stood still, the day Monica Smiley turned down a promotion from David Slaughter. She was chomping at the bit for a promotion. She was the top area manager, in the top store in the company, reporting to me at Meyerland Plaza in Houston. Everyone in my store and most other department managers in Palais Royal here in Houston knew she was first on the promotable list. After all, she was considered the best merchandiser in Houston, she was the one they always stole from my store to help go open new stores. After all, you had to go through my store as the last stop on your way to the top. I only took the best, trained the best, and promoted the best; what they did with it after that was all theirs.

My boss called and offered her the assistant manager position in Almeda Mall in Houston. I called Monica in to tell her of the great news. When I offered her the position with a nice raise, she looked me dead in my eyes and said, "No thank you, I have trained in this store under you, I came here to become a store manager, not an assistant manager so I will wait for a store to come open." Stunned, but elated, what Monica does not know until today, was that the level of respect she gained from me that day by saying no, was immeasurable. She was right; an area manager overseeing $2 million in a $10 million store need not be an assistant as they had already played that role managing the volume in a single department that most retailers oversee in an entire operation.

Truthfully, it was the same theory Bernard Fuchs had patterned with me: put the best performers, the highest potential people, in your best situations. Boy, did I feel stupid, but only for a moment. Interestingly, three weeks later, I received a second call from my boss, the same one that had called me back in Corpus eating some crow. This time, there was no crow eaten as he had figured it out on his own this time as she was promoted to Store Manager of the League City store. The lesson learned is huge. It is the same as the chapter "All you have to do is ask," by knocking. Sometimes you have to say no and you have to know when to say no. No is not always a bad thing, it just leads you through a different door of success. Monica will come up again in another chapter, but know: it is people like Monica Smiley that allow me to be right in the advice I provide you—great people make you successful.

I want to take you through my first promotion into a store manager position as we jump ahead now. I was an assistant manager in Lufkin, Texas where I had worked for four years back in the summer of 1989 when I received the call for a promotion on the exact same day I was spreading ten yards of dirt in my front yard. It was to be my first store manager position in Jasper, Texas, a town located near the piney woods of East Texas.

My store manager in Lufkin, Jerry Forrest, had prepared me a few minutes prior to the call that he thought I was going to receive an offer. For the next 30 minutes, I left my front door open as I began to move dirt as if I was a 275-pound construction worker preparing to lay the foundation for a new home. The call came shortly, I dashed inside and my life changed forever. Jasper was a town of 25,000 and as it turns out if you were the Bealls store manager; you were receiving the keys to "Mount Olympus." So, I was summoned by the Stage Stores Inc. gods while moving dirt one hot summer day in Lufkin, Texas. The manager I replaced left to manage a much larger store near Austin, called Round Rock. That is how it worked back in the day, you would throw your name in the hat for a bigger store and then you kept your fingers crossed that you were high enough on the promotable list, hoping you were in good enough standing with your district manager. Then you waited, waited, and waited for "the call." Eventually you made that first call to share the great news, meaning you got it. Or you heard through the grapevine someone else got it instead of you in which case you might say to yourself, "Oh well, got to get on the list early next time around," and back to work you would go. That process of promotions for Bealls was getting ready to change abruptly and I was going to become the symbol of that change for an entire company.

I arrived at my assignment in Jasper, Texas with eyes wide open to the major opportunities. This was not just your typical door to open. I always heard that your first store is the one you remember. I prefer doors you can open and close by yourself like Jasper, I like accessible doors of opportunity. Inside my first store manager door, I found a gold mine and it was clear at first glance that I had chosen the right door to enter. The store manager was a Greek God in the eyes of the community of Jasper. He had been president of the Jasper Lions Club and he was one of the cowboys that got to shoot 'em up at the OK Corral at halftime of the annual Jasper Rodeo, which was the biggest thing in Jasper, Texas—just ask Clint Black.

I discovered quickly that his store was running on autopilot because he was required to spend too much time out roaring with the Lions all the time and as a result, he had been allowing his employees to mine for gold on their own all too often. He had a good staff with a sharp, strong-willed assistant (that is putting it mildly) but they needed a captain, a leader that was present and accounted for. They needed a leader that would go with them into the mining tunnel each day, making sure it was still safe to mine, one that was always looking ahead to ensure the bigger pieces of gold were not overlooked.

Please do not misunderstand my intentions; the Jasper community loved this man, his results were great, and the sales he harvested because of his Lions Club participation and leadership in the Jasper community could not be disputed. In fact, in the eyes of these East Texas folks, this newcomer to their community was only a cub. I vividly recall receiving dirty looks my first few days, weeks, and months from some of the cliquish Jasper crowd as I began by taking his picture down at the front of the store replacing it with mine, as was our procedure. They were looks that communicated to me, "You might be the new manager trying to take his place, but you will never be him," as they smiled and shuffled on by me. As one of my punishments for not being their beloved main lion, I was required to operate the cotton candy booth at the Jasper rodeo that first year. As a lion in training, there would be no shoot-'em-up for me. In the end, they were right—I would never be him. What I would be someday was his boss when he reported to me as one of my fourteen district managers in my territory from 2003 until 2007 and honestly, he was one of the most consistent lions of the bunch. I guess that Jasper experience stuck with him, yippee ki yay!

It was so easy right from the start and yet I had thought it was going to be so very hard. Looking back on my transition from sales into properly managing my own store, I recall times when I had looked at the stars, wondering if just because I could beat everyone in sales, could I run the whole show myself? The answer was yes I can and I did just as you can do too. You have to learn the ropes, follow the rules, set the right example, and call someone you trust when you do not have the answer you need, and the rest will come in time. You may determine as I did in my first store that there are plenty of people who will help you succeed. For the most part, your employees know the ropes and if you treat them with respect, they will keep things running smoothly. Focus upon things you do as being the things that have the greatest potential to offer the best long-term result in your business or within your organization.

To be forthright with you, I cannot tell you how many times in managing one of my first three stores that I was asked a question I did know the answer to and my learned response would be, "Let me get back to you on that in a few minutes." Then I would go call Jerry Forrest, Bob Hart, or Ernie Cruse for advice. Only then, would my answer be guaranteed to be correct; I would now furnish the correct answer and I did not give my power away by providing a knee-jerk ego response without thinking it through. Most importantly, I continued to run my store the right way. Remember, all you have to do is ask and I just kept asking. I asked the right people, after all, they were the same people that had allowed me to learn by making mistakes at their own expense. Why would I worry about asking those questions prior to making a mistake in judgment or policy? Think about it, it is not brain surgery, it just made plain sense to me!

Bob Hart and Jerry Forrest should have received a portion of my salary those first few months for what they had instilled in me those first six years was what I relied upon, to succeed. I made repeated trips to my old store in Lufkin to borrow hardware, fixtures and other items to spruce the store up until finally Scott Foster, the assistant in Lufkin told me kindly but firmly one evening, "Uh, Mr. Forrest said not to let you have anything else." That was ok as my car was loaded and the truth be known, Mr. Forrest kept helping me and Scott kept looking the other way.

Almost every person had already warned me, "Do not change anything, Slaughter, go slow, and ease into it." By the way, that was the advice from the "Lion King," as he walked out of that door into a new world. No advice could have been so wrong. I changed everything. It is all in how you sell it and you sell it by gaining their respect, by talking to them, by working side by side with them. Employees watched as I made trip after trip to Lufkin personally hauling old things that made our little store look newer. All the while, they were observing my hard work, my commitment to my new assignment and my energy.

No doubt, the constant changes including reworking the floor, running around like a wild man most of the time—caused some of the employees and some of the Jasper folks to shrug their shoulders, but I didn't care. Despite a few negative folks, we were marching to a different drum. I simply stayed in the store all day and worked side by side with the employees. I earned their respect quickly as a result and I learned during the process that employees will climb mountains and move mountains in order to help you succeed when you ask them to do it with you, not because you say they have to do it. Your energy, your enthusiasm and your commitment to excellence cannot be underestimated and your employees are watching your every step.

In Jasper, I quickly dismissed the same criticisms and crap you hear about the previous store manager and I dismissed idle gossip about how he had not done this and not done that. The

"Major Opportunities"

store had done well under him so you have to take all of that with a grain of salt. My previous mentor Jerry Forrest had shown me the way when he spent no time wasted with idle gossip, no time spent ripping the old manager to pieces as the store was messed up when he got there. Instead, he walked bravely and confidently through his door of opportunity and he stayed inside the door allowing hard work, leadership, and store results to do all his talking.

Some years later when I flew in on the company plane for a Jasper store visit, despite the fact that it was not in my territory of responsibility, it was nice to walk the store again and see the house that we had built with the support of loyal, Jasper employees. Interestingly, one of my ex housekeeping employees happened to be in the store that day. What she said to me after not seeing her for all those years was touching and it has stayed with me. Her name is Sue and she is a remarkable mother and woman. I hired Sue to help me keep my store clean. She was already working three jobs, one with the school district, another somewhere else in Jasper, then she would come to the store in the evening to work in my store. In just two hours, each day Sue would do the work of three that it might take two hours each to accomplish. She never slowed down, she never once complained, and she never stopped working.

Sue said to me that day I visited, "Mr. Slaughter, I am so glad to see you again, I just wanted to tell you what I remember most about you was when you got here was when you and your son went into those nasty, dirty employee bathrooms." She went on to say, "I remember you just kept scrubbing those sinks and those filthy urinals, you cleaned those bathrooms, and then you painted both of them from top to bottom. I know now that you did that as much for us as employees and I wanted you to know, that's why I always respected you, I have never forgotten that about you, Mr. Slaughter." As I have already said once to you, "Do not ask anyone to do what you are not willing to do." As I got back on that company plane, I did so with a sense of pride, humbled in the knowledge that I do indeed still put my pants on just like everyone else and lest I forget that, that's what mattered to those who helped me up the mountains we had climbed together. By the way, Sue was correct, as those were some of the dirtiest restrooms I have seen—and I have not used CLR since and. I am still sore from that project but it worked and it still works today. People are watching so do not ask them to do, what you are not willing to do and then just head on up Mount Success.

Over the next year and a half, we raised the volume in Jasper from $2.2 million in annual sales to $2.9 million, or a 33 percent increase. We broke company records for opening new Bealls charge accounts, which was the lifeblood of business for our company. The first year I was in Jasper we went from opening a measly 300 accounts per year to over 2,300 new accounts. New charge accounts meant customers spent their hard-earned money that day and then of course, they came back repeatedly, especially in a small town where they had nowhere else to go shop. Bealls business grew over the years because small town folks are generally loyal to their town, as they prefer to keep their money in their town as the down to earth people that made my ex-company the place to shop in rural America, until this day.

Fortunately, as is supposed to happen in theory, someone would take notice of our incredible sales and charge account results and another door just might just come open for me. My district manager was Ernie Cruse. Ernie someday would take over the entire company and would promote me and another person, Pat Bowman, to Sr. VP has to run the company at his side, to fight our way out of bankruptcy with the company we all three loved dearly. Pat just recently retired from Stage Stores Inc. at age 55. The company was so lucky to have him for over 35 years as he was a company man, and he was a true leader in every sense of the word. They do not make leaders like Pat Bowman anymore, as he is cream of the crop and I learned so much from him over the years. He taught me to pay attention to details, to fight for what you believe in and occasionally, when to keep my mouth shut at a staff meeting, which he rarely chose to do but his heart was always in the right place. Ernie knew exactly what he was doing

"Major Opportunities"

when he put the two of us together. We were strong as one but we were stronger as two that worked as one.

Now, to that next opportunity door I said just might open. After about a year and a half in Jasper, Ernie took me aside during a store visit to tell me Mr. Fuchs, had instructed him to place me in the largest volume store he could find and to place him there as soon as he possibly could. Mr. Fuchs was preparing to make his mark on guidelines for promotions as he would be initiating significant changes in terms of promoting in a large company, and he began with me as his first risk in order to make the point he wanted to make. Boy, that sounded good to me but when might that happen, I wondered? Over coffee at McDonalds, Ernie made no concrete promises, he set no specific dates but he offered me a carrot of hope and inspiration as I headed back into the Jasper store, now sworn to secrecy. I now knew that someday soon, another door would open and that I needed to prepare myself for that and it was all the motivational charge I needed, and of course, Ernie knew that.

A few months later when most people thought there might be many names in the hat for this gigantic store, I received a call and another huge door of opportunity would open. Promoted to the Padre Staples Mall Bealls in Corpus Christi, Texas, I was moving from a $2.9 million dollar store to the third highest volume store in the chain doing $8 million in annual sales. It was a great phone call and a much bigger door, one you might be able to drive a moving van through, was getting ready to open wide. The same day I was promoted to the Corpus store, I received a call from the Jasper Lions Club to tell me they had voted me into office as the organization's secretary. Sadly, the previous roaring Lion club president informed me it was not an honor. My guess is they were still mocking me for not being worthy to walk in his shoes. It bothered me very little though when I told them I would have to pass on that promotion because I was moving on up, going to Corpus, to walk into another one of those "Major Opportunities."

My experiences in moving from a smaller volume store to a much higher volume store were exciting, overwhelming and monumental, all in one. I only knew methods I had learned along the way but everyone still offered the same lame old advice. They said to go slow, ease into it, sell yourself slowly, do not make changes at first, let them get to know you, blah, blah, blah, blah, wrong again, sports fans. No, instead I did it my way, the right way. I hit the floor running at a furious pace and I did not slow down for the next two years. As was the case in the Jasper promotion, I benefited from the fact that the previous store manager had also spent too much time out of his store as well. He was a group manager serving a leadership role among the other stores in Corpus, a training position to become a district manager. Accordingly, he too was not on the sales floor much. Again, the store had been running on auto-pilot but this time with an average management team at the helm.

The biggest change I recognized was in having more management due to the difference in volume, between the two stores. I discovered quickly that quantity is not necessarily better than quality as it pertains to defining a strong management team. I knew I needed to earn some respect very quickly, demand loyalty, and begin building a strong team of sales associates, who had "deer in the headlight" looks in their eyes for the first few days. I must admit it was overwhelming at first but I was like a kid in a candy store, the candy was plentiful and I love candy.

My resume now reflects the results we achieved in Corpus Christi, Texas for the two years I ran the store but what it does not tell is the story of how we accomplished it so quickly and so dominantly. The most important thing I changed from day one was to begin having productive store meetings, store manager meetings and a store mini-meeting every single morning, all led by me. I suspect the majority of the employees must have thought I was nuts for a while but then again they were hungry for some major changes. It was very clear to me that no one had been leading by example. I was the new flavor of the month in their life and they could see, hear and sense the enthusiasm in my walk, my talk and in my actions.

The most important concept I initiated was to find, develop, and maximize strong employees that I decided to term, "Top

Guns," which I will explain in detail in chapter nine. The larger the store, the more important it is that you develop key top productive, powerful, respected, driven, team leaders. They do not have to all be extroverts, they just have to be hungry for more, challenged more often, and praised and recognized on a daily basis. I needed to open some doors for them and to convince them to come inside and look around, I was sure they would want to stay.

Within the first four months, we had accomplished amazing feats of success. We began to experience bigger sales increases than the store had seen before. As a management team we were now committed to staying on the floor consistently due in large part to the fact I was there 100% of the time and we were obsessing upon the daily sales goal, upon beating the last year sales figures without fail. Third, we began to focus on new account production with a passion, the lifeblood of most retail stores, our proprietary charge card. Fourth, we re-merchandised the entire 50,000 square foot store, and that was a lot of hard work. Fifth, I made a deal with a local furniture storeowner and he agreed to supply some nice pieces of finished furniture placed strategically throughout the store in an effort to spruce up the store and to fill a big ugly box. I placed his company name professionally on each piece. It provided a new look in a large, boxy store and of course, it demonstrated to the staff that we could do anything and that I would.

I filled twenty-five open staffing bases that were empty prior to my arrival. The management team understood quickly that I was going to be in the store a lot, that I was going to stay on the floor most of the time and that the only captain of this ship was "Captain Dave." Our results began to set the pace for the district and eventually for the entire chain in all measurable results. Thankfully, after four months of hard work, Mr. Fuchs decided to bring a bus full of the buying division down from Houston with some executives from Bealls and Palais Royal. I suspect he wanted them to see first-hand why the store was suddenly bursting at the seams as reflected by results. I knew why it was happening and so did he. It was leadership 101; it was working side by side with caring employees that were excited, motivated and inspired.

As Mr. Fuchs walked the store in a stately, deliberate, confident manner, he stopped at the front of my store peering in the store in amazement. I stood at his side as he peered into my store, as he smiled at me and then shook my hand as a proud papa might do. He turned to my district manager Ron Stephens and said, "This is the best store we have in the company because it is where we have the best store manager, this is amazing, simply amazing Ron." That statement and that moment made the long hours, the hard work, worth it. Genuine, timely, heartfelt praise is critical and Mr. Fuchs dished out praise for the entire visit. I cannot take the credit for it, because it was a great team of employees with pride, who accomplished the task.

It was a great day for all of us, it was a not unlike a day I described for you in chapter one I attended. The employees were beaming with pride and it was a top of the mountain feeling that every store manager longs for. It demonstrates what can happen with leaders at the helm of motivated employees by developing a team with a sense of pride in themselves, in their cause and in their purpose. The extra merchandise we received was due to the buyers and was icing on the cake. I found out that on the way back to Houston Mr. Fuchs told the buyers to load us up with merchandise and that they did. The snowball was officially rolling and as a result, we enjoyed a healthy 12 percent increase that first year followed by a 17 percent increase the second year. It was an incredible journey and it is one that I will not forget. I will never stop thinking about those incredible people and I miss them to this day as they defined my success and my vision was their vision of success.

A Very Different Door Opens Next

The next big major opportunity door I knocked on and entered was not the door I thought it was going to be. By now, I was a group manager, a district manager in training. It had been a year and a half since I arrived and I was overseeing three of the other Corpus stores while managing my $9.6 million store in

"Major Opportunities"

Padre Staples Mall. The concept of serving as a group manager was flawed. I would be the first to admit I was a very good store manager but taking me out of the third highest store in the company producing in sales, made no sense at all. It caused me to operate as an average group manager, and it ran the risk of reducing my effectiveness as a store manager in one of the most important stores in the company. That role of responsibility would eventually be eliminated from the company altogether. Nevertheless, while playing both roles for six months or so I received a call that the Houston corporate office wanted to talk to me in Houston. At first, I allowed my ego to assume they might be offering me a district manager position but I knew in my heart I had not yet earned a promotion and I was definitely not ready for it. When they flew me to Houston, I thought I was knocking on one door; instead, it was a different one altogether.

As it turns out, the summon I received was to ask me to move back to Houston, back to my home to manage the top store in the company through a difficult six-month remodel. I would need to give up the group manager position, giving up the one path to becoming a vice-president. I was not sure this was the right door for me as it might push back a promotion still spinning in my head as the next big door I wanted to enter. Mr. Fuchs knew it would be a difficult task to manage this store—it was experiencing big losses already, it was an old beat up store so he insisted on placing his best store manager in his top store. He saw it as an honor as would I especially since he was a mentor.

When I arrived at the corporate office that morning, I was welcomed to Houston by being high-fived by Bealls executives Jim Hanks and John Crew and then left to sort out the details with the Palais Royal Senior VP., Mr. Smith #2. This would turn out to be a difficult meeting because I had made him look rather silly by having huge sales increases during my stay in the same mall in which his Palais Royal store was experiencing sales losses. To make matters worse, he had been drug to Corpus to see my store and Mr. Fuchs had rubbed it in his face. On top of that hurt, Mr. Fuchs now informed him I would take over his top store. It was uncomfortable for both of us especially for him as we sat down to iron things out. He told me the salary would be a modest nine percent yearly increase. He said I needed to report immediately and that he wanted me to co-manage the store with the 40-year tenured Palais Royal manager who was retiring in a few months. I thought to myself, "Are you kidding me? I am not a co-manager and I change things on my own."

Instead, in a soft-spoken voice, I asked three questions; first, "Is the salary negotiable?" I was from Houston, I did not expect gold, frankincense, and myrrh but it was worth inquiring about. Second, I told him my wife was pregnant with our third child (Kaitlyn) and I would prefer to finish the year in Corpus Christi and have the baby with my wife's personal doctor. I asked if the move could wait until the baby was born in December. Third, I let him know politely that I am not a co-manager by design but I kept to myself it was not the style I had grown accustomed to and was certainly not a door I had a desire walk through. "Mr. Smith #2," listened without saying a word and then with a slightly reddened face, in an almost scolding tone, certainly dismissive, he said, "Those are the terms David." I smiled a fake half-smile and told him I would visit with my wife when I got back to Corpus and I would get back with him.

Ironically, I was sitting in the exact same office that one day I would occupy, someday to have his job, I would sit in the same chair as Senior Vice President of Stage Stores Inc. He was sitting inside my door of major opportunity, in my chair, and neither of us knew it. Doors have a strange way of opening, closing and then opening again someday. "Be careful how you treat people on your way to the top," I remember Jerry Forrest saying, "Some of them are on their way down." Interestingly, it was the same advice that he would offer me in a card I received after he "retired," a few years later. Actually, Mr. Smith #2 was a classy man, a family man who was not part of the master plan to organize, grow, and maximize soon to be one of the better retail companies in the country.

"Major Opportunities"

Dejected and confused, I boarded a plane back to Corpus and by the time I walked back into my store, I received a phone call. It was same Mr. Smith #2, but this time his tone was different. He said he had visited with Mr. Fuchs, the CEO. While sounding slightly muffled on the phone as if he was eating some crow, he said Mr. Fuchs had agreed that my salary should be higher (15%). Second, Mr. Fuchs had agreed I should finish the year and have our baby in Corpus Christi, Texas in December. Third, he agreed David Slaughter was not a co-manager type and that I could report the same day the retiring store manager was to leave. All objections resolved, I accepted the position he offered immediately and I would then be given the keys to my biggest door yet — one block from where I grew up for 17 years in Bellaire, Texas, I went home.

A few years later, I went to visit Mr. Fuch's shortly before his departure from the company to thank him for what he had done for me, for what he had taught me and to say goodbye. That day he clarified that, the trip to Houston was all part of my master plan. He told me he thought I had been a great store manager and an average group manager. He said I needed to continue to grow but that he was sure I would do well. He was right about me being an average group manager. He said he knew I would do well and he wished me good luck.

Great mentors and great visionaries like Bernard Fuchs find a way to keep high potential people promoting into the most important stores and positions in an organization. They do not make management decisions based solely upon seniority. Great mentors are not preoccupied with their position, their status or with individual success. Instead, they focus upon getting the best person into the most important spot and they put their money where their mouth is. Mr. Fuchs was a wonderful leader and Stage Stores Inc. lost a brilliant man when he decided to retire and in my mind, we were never the same after that.

Who is your Mentor?

~ *Chapter 5* ~
Mentoring 101:Learning & Teaching

Early in my career I suspect I was like many other aspiring salesmen because I believed I could beat anyone on any given day but what I did not know was whether or not I could make the necessary transition into management and still be highly successful. That kind of transition requires a different set of traits and success is largely contingent upon acquiring and utilizing strong people skills in order to succeed through others. People can learn how to manage others but typically, there are very few who master it at a level allowing them to get to the top in any large company. Arguably, it takes the right mix of desire, skill, time spent with good mentors. It requires practical application applied to your management style in order to build a team of people capable of going to the top of a mountain with you as the leader.

In this chapter, I will attempt to support the notion that mastering success by getting to the top in any sales profession has to do with the mentors you find, with the decisions you make and how you apply what you learn along the way into establishing your style of management. As I reflect upon my retail career in clothing, I easily draw upon four men that served as mentors to me. All four had previously mastered a high level of success throughout their retail careers by applying their talent and skill set including a high level of intelligence, style, charisma, organizational skills, and a unique ability to teach others. All four of these men had one thing in common — they were great teachers.

Bob Hart

The first mentor, Bob Hart, afforded me an opportunity to master my sales skills while learning retail management 101 skills through the process of watching him. The second one, Jerry Forrest my store manager in Lufkin, Texas would teach me how to maximize profit, how to turn a business around quickly and how to treat people fairly. The third, Ernie Cruse would serve as my boss for the seven most prosperous years of my career as a Sr. VP at Stage Stores Inc . . . He taught me how to build to stay built and how to do it without micromanaging. The fourth mentor was Bernard Fuchs and he would change the life of many as he led the merger of two great companies developed into one.

I wanted to share some of the common dominant characteristics present in these mentors. I hope in doing so, you can begin to identify some of these same traits in your boss and in your key relationships. My purpose in sharing their influence upon me is to encourage you to find your influential person in life and then to soak up all of the mentoring you can obtain from them. Your circle of influence plays a significant role in your success. I also hope I can convince you to become a mentor to another as passing it on makes for meaningful life work and can become something you can hold up with pride.

Let me begin with Bob Hart, the example I provided for you in "All you have to do is ask as he is the one I first asked for a job, the one I asked to take me with him to Tyler. This part of the story starts at the point in time he had taken me to Tyler to begin a management career as a manager trainee. As I alluded to earlier, Bob Hart's management style was based upon, "Only do what only he could do." By that, I do not mean to imply he was not a leader or that he did not put in his share of hard work. Instead, I am referring to what Mr. Hart mastered over the years including an uncanny ability to maximize the strength and talents of others while maintaining a tight reign over his store operations. Bob was the very best customer service manager I have ever met. He knew when to be in his office but more importantly, he knew when to stay on the floor. When there was peak business, Bob was on the floor. I learned from him that every manager must have a floor presence. Bob could be on the sales floor yet aware of exactly what was occurring on the opposite side of the store. He did not stop what he was doing; it was usually the most important thing he could be doing. Instead, he taught by his presence and by his example on the sales floor that it mattered he was visible on the floor by sales associates and by customers, consistently.

Bob Hart never tired of customers and his legendary reputation for opening doors for customers, helping them out to their car with packages and his ability to look them in the eye with his smile, resulted in many happy return customers in Tyler, Texas. Bob Hart was a businessman first and his ability to see across the store and get to that spot eventually was equally manifested in his ability to speak demonstratively about the unacceptable condition of a department or something that was supposed to have been taken care of that had been missed. He did not miss much that was going on in his store.

It seems necessary for me to provide some advice pertaining to career moves, promotions and advancement. Often, an aggressive individual will jump at a chance for promotion for the sake of advancement and one of my goals in writing this book is to encourage you to go slow, carefully evaluating each career move from a short term and a long-term perspective. Many things have changed over the years but one that has not changed is the impact of one bad move gone wrong or one opportunity that goes unfulfilled because someone prematurely threw away their learning experience while exposed to a great mentor. I will provide examples in subsequent chapters to explain what I mean. Call it luck, call it perception, call it timing, but my successful career had more to do with staying where I needed to be not being afraid to turn a promotion down at the expense of growing in a position or developing under a great mentor for the long term like a Bob Hart.

In Tyler, the expectations were high from the very beginning. Tyler had been waiting for a Bealls since the Garden of Eden and when the Tyler founding fathers finally granted permission for Bealls to come in, Bob Hart jumped at the opportunity. When Bob took my wife and I to Tyler with him it was a fresh start for both of us. Both sets of parents lived in Houston and were loving families but it did give us a start on our own that I highly recommend to any newlyweds for high consideration. I vividly recall my competitive nature even as I was sweeping sawdust off a new floor the first few days in Tyler with little more to do in the unfinished store. I remember walking up and down, stalking, meticulously pacing the floor in an effort to understand and prepare for how far someone selling in the other adjacent men's department would have to come to compete with my sales or as I saw it, to steal a sale. It is quite possible it was out of some sense of insecurity but it would become preparation for a drive to the top in sales I did not know was ahead yet. As I reflect, I suspect I was trying to compensate for a feeling of inadequacy not having completed the college degree I had squandered back in 1983.

We were on commission in those days and although there was a small management salary, our income came by producing outstanding sales results. I knew I wanted to win, I knew winning meant possible reward through promotion, it was perceived as a sign that one had management potential which all required showing up on the sales report each month. I had tasted some success by making the report while in Houston but it had only wet my appetite for blood. Tyler would become the vehicle for individual sales success for me but what I am most grateful for is the exposure I received to one of the finest management teams assembled.

Bob Hart introduced us newbie 'management trainees to an understanding of the interviewing and hiring process in search of what he termed "Keepers." Bob put people through several intense interviews, a process that was interesting to watch un-fold.

In any type of retail business, you are only as good as the people you choose to surround yourself with and Bob Hart was a master at finding great people. The staff he assembled to open Tyler Bealls in 1983, was the best I have seen. He made hiring decisions based upon what was "a good fit" for each individual department. It was like a jigsaw puzzle and Bob Hart was putting the pieces that fit together to complete this puzzle on time.

These days too many companies settle for less than what they can get when it comes to staffing their business for reasons including; not having enough time to screen them, or they needed them yesterday, or turn-over is ongoing and is accepted as normal. Other reasons include payroll pressures forcing a store to be unable to compete with prevailing wages in their market, or allowing a subordinate to decide what a good hire is, they may not know or may not been taught the true definition. Mr. Hart relied upon himself and his experienced, hand selected assistant Mike Mayfield to make all final decisions but he exposed us to the process from the very beginning. It helped us comprehend that he wanted only the very best and to see what the best looked like, assembled as a team, was very powerful.

Another way Bob Hart affected me is that he taught me it was important to be consistently fair. Although I remember him fondly as a father figure, as a loving, unselfish, demanding, yet kind man, perhaps what I remember most is that he insisted that you have to treat people fairly and apply that with consistency. He did not play favorites among employees as people often do in business consciously or subconsciously today. Although the other management trainees accepted that as his sr. manager trainee, summoned to follow, he made sure he treated us the same. He enforced the rules the same in their presence with me as he did any of them. I vividly recall the time he was getting ready to reprimand one of the other manager trainees for gross violations of tardiness.

As Mr. Hart was preparing for the counseling session with the offending trainee, he went into the office and checked all of our management time cards for punctuality. Amazingly, despite never taking a lunch, always remaining on the sales floor, I too was apparently guilty as well of punching in a few minutes late all too often. He did address the issue one on one with the biggest violator as his first priority but he also called me back into his office in time and addressed my need to be on time as well. He told me was surprised to discover that I too had an issue with following the policy by punching in consistently. Like a whipped puppy spanked by his master, I obediently fell into place, limping off to lick my wounds having learned the lesson of treating everyone the same is not something that is negotiable. The one you reprimand most severely must be treated the same as the one that might be your favorite. Given this example early on, impartiality was an ingredient I applied throughout my career. Too many lawsuits, discrimination upheavals and mediations occur by not enforcing the rules the same on everyone, no matter who they might be and businesses could benefit by applying the Bob Hart rule of treating everyone the same.

    Bob Hart was a great teacher. We always had management meetings, as those were never optional. How many times have you sat in an unproductive time waster called a management meeting? The definition of a great meeting is not contingent upon the kind of pastry or donut made available for human consumption, despite what you have heard or what you may have eaten. We were required in Bob Hart's training sessions to contribute to the conversation while eating. Much like a bible schoolteacher going through the Holy Bible itself, he was meticulous in his teaching habits. It was a retail bible he was very familiar with—book, chapter and verse. Bob Hart systematically taught from this bible of retail sales, exposing us from week to week to a lesson centered on driving business, improving profit and making retail fun.

    Management meetings have become somewhat outdated in today's world I fear, which is a mistake. Well planned, well-executed meetings still have a place in shaping the success of retailers. Fun should always be at the forefront of any morning meeting, mini-meeting or store meeting. Nordstrom management is renowned for their ability to create a spark in a matter of only fifteen to twenty minutes in a morning kick off or rally with their employees. It is not about the length of the meeting, it is about getting the day started in an up-beat way, every single day. We had a morning meeting in my two hundred stores every single morning. Even as employees straggle in, and the front door has to be opened, locked and reopened several times, a good start to the day is still basic in the retail environment. The extent to which management sets as a priority to make it fun by getting blood flowing from the first part moment of the morning has a huge impact on how successful the results will be for that. The management meetings, the store meetings and the morning mini meetings that were conducted in Tyler were motivating, instructive and long lasting and today's retail teams can benefit from a similar plan

Finally, Mr. Hart taught me something I would never forget, a lesson relevant in today's business environment. He taught me not to get rid of someone until there is a plan to replace him or her ... That sounds easy enough but I had to learn it the "Hard" way or should I say the "Hart" way, a lesson learned at the expense of having to wipe egg off my face one Saturday morning in Tyler, Texas. I had just about had it with a top shoe sales-woman in the Tyler shoe department let us call her, Mrs. Smith, no relation to Mr. Smith number one or number two by the way; it was time for her to get a lesson in sales. By that I mean she wasn't willing to be run over like a freight train and cower to the domination of my ability to work faster and smarter, so she deliberately, purposely, stole a large sale of mine smiling from ear to ear at me as she did it. Now that was a mistake, a big mistake. Therefore, I decided to go on offense. I began to take every sale, mine, her's, anyone's, everyone's; just to make a point that I could shut her down completely and boy did I shut her down. I was rude, arrogant, and unfair and I got in her face, on purpose. I think at one point I had $2700 in sales to her $175 including the $75 sale she had stolen from me to begin with, a $75 pair of grey, men's, Bill Blass shoes in case you think I forgot. After about four hours of this full court press, she finally threw up her hands, muttering to herself as I recall saying, "I can't do this anymore, and I give up." She marched abruptly to the back and promptly told Mr. Hart she could not work with me anymore, she would be quitting with no notice and she was done. Shortly there-after, I was cordially invited over the loud speaker to come to Mr. Hart's office where behind closed doors, he taught me a lesson I would always remember. Kindly but sternly, he helped me understand that she too was a top performer in his store, that he understood that clearly there were issues but he wanted to know what my plan for replacing her sales starting the next day would be since I was in charge of his entire shoe department.

Opening my mouth to say something, to say anything, produced nothing. My mouth opened but my voice remained silent for I knew I had no plan; that she did sell a lot and she was a solid shoe sales woman. He never once raising his voice and I fully understood the "Hart" way—that there is a time to deal with staffing issues, perhaps even a time to draw a line in the sand but that you never want to put yourself (him) in a position where you have no plan, left without a solution. I apologized as I thought he wanted me to do and he suggested kindly that perhaps I was apologizing to the wrong person. I went back out on the floor to apologize and to eat some humble pie myself. She reluctantly accepted my genuine apology and then we went on that day to have a record day in shoe sales as we worked through our differences just fine until promoted a few months later. He was right and I was wrong, even though I still enjoyed beating her like a wild monkey that day in sales. The exercise taught me to think ahead in terms of personnel weaknesses and needs in any one of my stores. Before he went home that evening, from a phone across the store, he called the shoe department and said, "Dave, I am proud of you, you grew a lot today, you came a long way today young ma." My stubborn, selfish, hurt feelings dissolved very quickly after that call. The man I looked to as a father was trying to teach me a painful lesson that he had learned so long ago.

I could write for many more pages about what I learned in two years under Bob Hart but I will end by saying that if any of you are so lucky as to have a Bob Hart in your life, keep him there, and soak it up like a sponge. Watch him, listen to him, and begin to mimic his behavior as best you can because that behavior is to become the fragrance of the sweet smell of a life-time of success. As a side note, Tyler is where Bob Hart introduced me to an up and coming district manager named Ernie Cruse. Years later Ernie would go on to become my boss for those seven years when I was in charge of 200 plus stores at Stage Stores Inc. My introduction to Ernie included Bob literally dragging him over to praise me for exceeding $100,000 in sales for the month of December in 1984. Bob was full of pride and Ernie was a brilliant, no-nonsense company man, destined some-day to take the reins of Stage Stores Inc. when we were fighting for our lives in bankruptcy from 2000-2002, only to emerge under his leadership as textbook for emerging from bankruptcy. Ernie would become the glue that would keep a great company stuck together for a very long time.

Jerry Forrest

The second mentor I want to tell you about is a man named Jerry Forrest. My first promotion out of the Tyler store was to be area manager in Lufkin, Texas. For this native Houstonian, Lufkin was a different cup of tea altogether. Although I am grateful for the four years I spent in Lufkin, it is not one of my favorite vacation spots. Because I was one of the top paid commissioned sales people in the Bealls chain, when they called to offer me my first promotion into management, the HR manager informed me I would receive a salary of $21,000 and said that I needed to report effective immediately. "So, let me get this straight," I thought to myself, "I am making $26,000 a year as a sales man and I will be accepting a promotion losing $5,000 annually and my wife would lose her banking job as well?" Yes, that is right; sometimes to get to the top you have to be willing to go down. I recall on my first day in the Lufkin store calling my wife who would be moving soon with our belongings literally near tears, telling her on the

"Major Opportunities"

phone that this was the worst decision we could have made, that I was sorry, that I was quite certain I had ruined our lives. She remained a constant support, we did make the move and I was wrong, it was a great move. Sometimes doors are not what they appear to be and often you have to get comfortable inside your door of opportunity in order to find improved doors to enter.

Shortly after arriving in Lufkin, the store manager retired and the company brought Jerry Forrest into my life. Jerry had previously managed the number one profit store in Mt. Pleasant, Texas and had developed a reputation for driving sales while maximizing profit, which is a great formula for success. Jerry hit the floor running, cleaning up a mess, while inheriting a burned out assistant manager who was on his second or third marriage, loved alcohol more than most and did not understand the definition of punctuality. Quickly, Jerry sized up the situation, went straight to work and put his profit Midas touch on the store, changing literally everything. I recall Jerry playing Zig Ziglar tapes over the loud speaker before the store opened in the mornings, which I loved by the way. I also recall his assistant manager would go in his office and shut (slam) the door in an attempt to, "Shut that positive crap up," I think I heard him say one hang-over morning. Unfortunately, he was also shutting (closing) an opportunity door for himself, slamming the door on his future success, which would open a big door for me. Eventually, he was shipped to Enid, Oklahoma, disguised as a promotion, similar in retail terms to being banished to somewhere in Siberia.

In the four years I worked for Jerry Forrest, I learned a lot about business but more about doing the right thing by employing positivism. I credit what I learned from him as becoming the style of management I employed consistently on my way to the top. Jerry worked fast, smart and managed his time effectively, never tiring of breaking a sweat. He did not ask you to do anything he was not willing to do. His listening skills were the best I have seen and his loyalty to those that worked hard for him was unparalleled. I turned down a promotion early on because I wanted to stay and learn from Jerry. I made the right decision to stay in Lufkin and my time with Jerry would become a catalyst to my survival and high level of success as a new store manager and would lead to my success in running the two largest stores in the chain down the road.

It was about this time that Bealls and Palais Royal began the process of merging into one company. Lufkin was hand-picked as one of three test stores selected to study and understand how to create and employ best practices by taking the best of both companies to mold them into one company by a visionary, a brilliant CEO named Bernard Fuchs. He decided to test Palais Royal merchandise assortments in three Bealls stores and in the end, this six month study would confirm that rural markets had money in their pockets too and that they too appreciated quality career merchandise just as much as the next guy or girl did in metro markets. This presented me the major opportunity to learn the Palais Royal system that would help me achieve a full understanding of the merger of two companies into one. Jerry would be the mentor that kept the ship balanced, as we were tried and tested as a Bealls store operating as a Palais Royal store simultaneously for those six months. It was his positive, can do attitude.

What I learned from Jerry Forrest was significant and is still so completely relevant to the success one can enjoy in today's retail environment. First, I learned that you have to be careful how you treat people. Jerry set me down and told me something that has stayed with me until this day. He told me it was clear to him I was heading to the top at a very fast pace. Instead of being jealous like many do or protective of their shared knowledge, Jerry chose to impart with all of his knowledge and his experience, openly and freely. He explained to me that day that he wanted me to be careful of how I treated people on my way to the top. He told me that I needed to remember that as I was going up in the company that some might be coming down, some would be jealous; some would not understand my success and my drive that he observed on a daily basis. It was good advice that I tried to keep in the back of my mind going forward.

"Major Opportunities"

I submit that many a top executive chooses at some point to put on their pretend robe of royalty, sometimes forgetting that it is those at the bottom of their food chain, those who most often are responsible for the greatest good accomplished, and for most of the successes in a company, that are often forgotten first. Employees refer to this as, "they have changed. "Sometimes, they may fail or falter, never really understanding that we all put our pants on the same way each day, never really comprehending that how you treat your people, especially the higher you get, has a direct impact upon your desired results that you seek. Jerry still applies those same principles he taught some twenty-five years ago and to no surprise to me, he still succeeds every single day at the highest levels. As I finished editing my book, I learned that jerry finally retired a few months ago. Stage Stores Inc. lost a great leader, a great man and a great mentor. Somehow, I do not see Jerry Forrest as slowing down though I suspect he will just keep on teaching others and living a good life.

On a personal note, I have determined over the years that some people are truly happy just being mediocre, resisting change altogether, until it is literally forced upon them. Many of the very same people that do not want success are the same ones that can impede success for an entire team. The lessons Jerry was trying to teach me were much bigger than just humility, it went deep into recommendations about how to lead a team in the same direction of success. This acceptance of mediocrity, this type of stinky thinking is capable of becoming a cancer capable of killing an entire department, store, district or company. Left untreated, mediocrity breeds mediocrity and stores eventually close never realizing that the cancer was even there. Fortunately, this retail cancer has a cure, it just requires consistent doses of positive can—do medicine. Jerry brought the medicine he needed and I watched as he delivered huge doses throughout the four years I worked with him in Lufkin, Texas

Years later, Jerry Forrest left the company during bankruptcy. He purchased a plot of land in Lufkin and literally began building custom homes; he built a house from scratch by himself, to sell.

The market soured for home sales and in 2001, when placed in charge of fourteen districts in the company guess who I sought out to become one of my district manager's in one of the highest volume Houston districts. You got it, Jerry Forrest, the man who taught me how to make profit, drive sales and to build from the bottom up. The point he had made to me years prior, to be careful how you treat people on the way to the top had proven true. I always treated him with the utmost of respect and, admiration as I grew into my new roles with Stage Stores Inc. Jerry recently retired from Stage Stores Inc. and he will be missed most certain.

He allowed me to learn through mistakes made at his expense, even deferring occasionally to his wisdom of experience, choosing sometimes to purposely defer to my young and inexperienced passion. He never minced words in giving performance evaluations. We will touch on reviews, counseling and performance feedback in another chapter but Jerry did what a great leader does in evaluating his people, and he was honest, thorough and motivating in a review of your performance. Many times over those years in retail, I observed reviews conducted centered upon what happened last or what they remember most recently instead of relying upon proper preparation as the preferred method. Instead, Jerry used this quality time with you to provide honest, objective feed-back, always offering realistic hope for the future while he himself taking part by actively participating in a plan of action to help you move on along the career path you aspired to have. A review with Jerry was usually an hour long and included an uninterrupted review of your strengths; including opportunities to improve, all finalized in ink with a plan for next year's growth. It was our time to plan for future success and to discuss new doors to be, opened.

Ernie Cruse

The third mentor is Ernie Cruse. Ernie was not your typical man as he has a photo-static memory. In his humble way, he will not admit to that but Pat and I know it to be true. You may think having a flawless memory is a good thing but sometimes, it is not. It always made him catch the line missed in any document, always there as he said it was, but it caused us to become careful at digesting what we read, especially before we brought it up in a staff meeting.

Ernie is the single greatest reason Stage Stores Inc. emerged successfully from bankruptcy as a textbook retail success story. He retired in 2010 after forty-four years with the same company he started with as a young man. Ernie, a self-made man and a modern day example proving beyond a doubt that a person can reach the top of any company if they work hard, work smart and if they do it through developing great people. Returning to the photo static memory part, that thought still haunts me sometimes at night when I awake from a dream, grateful as I reach a sweaty realization that my nightmare is not real and that I can go back to sleep with no store visit scheduled the next day.

Ernie was promoted by the board of directors during bankruptcy to take the reins of a company that had grown entirely too fast, become too fat and had become leveraged at the expense of two sixty-year old established "branded," companies called Palais Royal and Bealls. Ernie was commissioned with the primary task of rebuilding what we had previously built, merged, and then had been destroyed by greed and some bad decision-making. It is not a new story, as it is one recounted throughout the history of retail. It is a sad story of companies that grow too quickly, too fast in order to please investors, stockholders and a greedy market. The pressures to match expectations set on the street each quarter may be masked in steady store growth and acquisitions, but for only so long. Eventually, the street gets wise to your plan; wise to the deception, wise to a simple miscalculation or a bad forecast you are reluctant to admit to in a conference call, prior to an earnings release. The stock goes up when you are thriving but it can come down at an alarming rate when you miss the numbers as badly as Stage Stores Inc. eventually did. As a result, the stock plummets back down to earth with a thud called panic. The harsh reality of demolition and rebuilding we call bankruptcy became a certainty creating great anxiety for 12,000 employees, as the hopes and dreams of the company you have given your heart and soul to for so long, becomes volatile.

It was sad to watch, some folks left broken, and some left broke. By that time, Pat Bowman and I had reached a level of regional manager and we were supervising districts of our own under the direct supervision of two sr. V.P.'s. We were about to walk through a huge door and we did not even know it. Uncertainty, panic, anger and confusion were prevalent throughout the chain during this crisis; it was time for Jim Scarborough and Ernie Cruse to take the reins of a company struggling to survive complete ruin.

Right away, Ernie had to make tough decisions but he proved up for the task. To Jim Scarborough's credit, he understood that Ernie would protect the stores. Jim was a strong merchant, which was critical to our recovery. The relationships that Jim had built over the years, the credibility and reputation that he brought to the Stage Stores Inc. table, is un-questionable. He has a charisma that is striking from the moment you meet him. Ernie loved the company with all of his heart, he was determined to save it, and Jim knew that too. Ernie's method, not unlike his own would be defined by making sound, well thought out financial decisions, always placing the jobs of the 12,000 employees the board entrusted him with as paramount. He understood what many at the top often forget, that success in a company starts and ends with the store staffing, store support and with store morale, not with a corporate office.

As a regional manager, I was traveling in Taos, New Mexico to the wonderland of barren land and cold tundra to visit some of my stores. My mind was drifting with the uncertainty of a door of opportunity gone awry. Reminded that I did not possess a college degree, with a fifteen year commitment to my one and only company, with four small children and a wife that had moved everywhere for my career, I was perplexed and quite concerned. I was pondering what I might do next if the axe came down on my family, so I was in a real quandary. Fortunately, the call that would push me through the next door of opportunity came on the road to Taos, New Mexico. Ernie Cruse asked Pat and I to be on a conference call in which he informed us he was only keeping the two of us, that the company was reorganizing the stores in a good faith effort to save our beloved company. He said it was not going to be easy but that we could do it, that we had to do it. Of course, we were elated, not yet fully understanding what all that meant other than we were safe for the moment without really knowing his solid plan to save Stage Stores Inc. from complete ruin.

Ernie kept us grounded on that phone call by clarifying that the two senior vice presidents, our current bosses, might have difficulty accepting, even understanding his decision to release them from their executive responsibilities. He assured us he had thought it through carefully and that he had every confidence in the two of us as the ones to lead the stores going forward. He explained that he had to make the decision he thought best for the future of the company as we made our attempt to return from bankruptcy. He also mentioned something he would remind us of several times in the next years that was important for us all to remember, that we better not screw this up for him.

During the final stages of preparing this book, one of those two previous bosses, John Crew, passed away at the age of 67. Although I did not mention him in the mentoring chapter, I probably could have written a whole chapter about John. He taught me so much about business, about professionalism, about maintaining character and dignity and about having fun along the way. It is sad that the world lost John Crew because he is one of the most special men I have ever met. Replacing him was no easy task as they were gigantic shoes to fill.

One can read about Stage Stores Inc., as that information can be located easily so feel free to find the story. It is a good read about what not to do and what to do. We went on to become a textbook example for how to emerge successfully from a highly leveraged bankruptcy. I am proud to say that the company now does over $1.6 billion now in thirty-eight states with over 850 stores at the printing of this first edition. Stage Stores Inc. is a source of income in 2013 and although a strong buying division, a solid loss prevention team, the store employees at store level, can share the credit for that fact perhaps the credit for the vision and the execution of that vision belongs mostly to Ernie Cruse and Jim Scarborough. I will mention Jim's role in the next chapter when I discuss the changes we made as we successfully emerged from bankruptcy, but as the new CEO, Jim had as a herculean task, to avoid a disaster of titanic proportion. Interestingly, one of the key people in charge of the stores when Stage Stores Inc. went into bankruptcy, Steve Lovell, eventually found his way back into his own major opportunity and is now the CEO of an up and coming company headquartered in Houston called Charming Charlie. He is a brilliant man and where one door may have closed for him amidst a crisis at Stage Stores Inc., another door opened at Charming Charlie. People like Steve, always make it to the top as they are destined to lead others to the top.

When I reflect upon what I learned from my third mentor, it begins with what he taught pertaining to store visitation. Ernie cared deeply about store staffing and about store personnel. He understood that it is the employees at store level that make the company work well, not a central office. We were there to support the stores as the first priority and his philosophy remained consistent throughout his reign at Stage Stores Inc. When we visited one of our stores with him, which was often, Ernie never openly lost his cool, he never resorted to yelling and throwing fits as you and I have seen happen all too often. He was the consummate professional. Do not get me wrong, there were butt whippings in the car, on the plane, at the restaurant, walking to the car, walking from the car to the store, walking from the car to the hotel, and walking from the hotel to get back in the car. He always did it in private where he could make his point without throwing his weight around unnecessarily. Ernie also let it go, he mentioned it and moved on and that separates him from most top executives that I am aware of in retail. He made his point, clearly and then moved on. He did not continue to beat a dead

"Major Opportunities"

horse until it is dead. Entirely too many upper management and executives cannot seem to let go of misgivings or mistakes made by a subordinate, they cannot let you forget it; they have to keep sticking it in from time to time. Too often, it seems they have to keep reminding you that they are that much smarter than you are when the truth is, you are gaining on them every single day. Ernie taught us that it was okay to make a mistake but that you needed to make a different one the next time.

Over those seven years under Ernie Cruse, the wisdom I gained in decision-making was a direct result of learning from my mistakes, at Ernie's expense and from professional coaching from Ernie. It is sound advice for any aspiring upward bound student of retail 101; you will make mistakes but next time, make a different one and learn from what you do wrong. Then, years later when you appear to be a genius to others, remember, it happened to you because you made a lot of mistakes and instead of acting all high and mighty, offer some understanding, some support and even some compassion demonstrating to those that you rely upon to deliver your own successes, from day to day.

Second, Ernie Cruse was a mathematical genius. Setting aside the fact that he was a walking road map, Ernie understood the analytics of sound financial planning and of allocation of services and goods due in large part to his previous job in the company as being in charge of planning and allocations. He was obsessed with this aspect of the business; always making sure, the stores were taken care of first in specific product needs, always keeping as a priority, catering to the specific needs of their individual market. If Ernie did lose his cool, it was because someone not listening to a store's opinion concerning their individual needs or not giving the stores ample ammunition in their arsenal of weapons called soft goods, or when they did something stupid.

Third, Ernie was the most effective executive I have worked with in terms of utilizing staff meetings in order to reach consensus, while maintaining and balancing his commitment to do the right thing by the company for the employees. He made it clear to Pat and me when he selected us to lead the stores that we had better pay close attention to what we do and that we darn sure better give strong consideration to studying the implications of decisions we might render. According to Ernie, the jobs and the livelihood of tens of thousands of hard working employees rested upon our shoulders. He made sure we clearly understood that they would be directly affected by most decisions we would make, and that we need not forget that. He loved the people that ran the stores, they loved and respected him, and they all depended upon him.

Although Ernie was usually always one step ahead at most every turn, he could be persuaded to reach a different point of view but the argument had to be well thought out, it had to be tested and proven before it was to be rolled out to a chain of 600 plus stores and on that notion, he was unmovable. He spent company money as if it were his own. He believed in spending the budget, otherwise he warned you might not have it to lose. He taught Pat and me to run a large company the same way when business was bad as we did when it was good. Too many companies, he warned, waste money in the best of times and are too tight in the worst of times. Ernie had his hands on everything, but he allowed us to run the stores.

Ernie taught us not to micromanage our district managers. A better way to say it is he broke me of a very bad habit. He sat me down early on in my tenure as an executive reminding me that I was responsible for the growth and development of fourteen high-powered district managers. He forced me to come to grip with a fact that many leaders tend to forget. He reminded me that when I was a store manager, maybe even as a district manager, I probably could get away with being a control freak and micromanaging my store or stores. What he taught me, painfully I must admit at times, was that I had to allow my direct reports the opportunity to breathe, to make mistakes and to learn from them, as Ernie would allow Pat and me to do. Strangely, even though my return university experience has been almost perfect, I did see one example that reminded me of this retail private sector truth. Even a great professor has to let go sometimes. Micromanaging

"Major Opportunities"

a qualified, enthusiastic, well-trained student will backfire on you. Way too many great people can be lost in any organization because the one in charge cannot, will not let go, allowing others to succeed on their behalf.

Ernie taught me that one of my main jobs was to maintain my own focus by keeping as a primary focus, keeping up with the unique growth needs from district Manager to district Manager, within my territory of 200 stores. It was a focus on keeping up with the growth, by developing people, to be better than myself. The result of consistent staffing, he knew, would always be tied back to comp sales increases and credit solicitation, both the lifeblood of the company. Ernie taught us that we needed to have a "Bob, the Builder," mentality. His definition of a successful builder, defined by removing the builder from the completed project and validating it stayed built proving only then that you have built something worth bragging about. For Ernie, that meant that a store or district continued to operate at the same high level you had been beating out of them all along. It took a while to comprehend his philosophy and to apply this well-founded strategy. I suspect it also required some calculated patience from him, but it always worked but it was the right strategy for success as we re-built a great company called Stage Stores Inc. that has remained strong now for 13 years

Lastly, Ernie taught Pat and me that we are always a direct reflection of the people we hire and of the hiring decisions, we make. He believed in having depth, we referred to that as bench strength. We relied upon a depth chart, discussed from week to week, from month to month with district managers and store managers alike. He insisted we must take full accountability for bad decisions we might make yet we must be prepared to move on, learning from personnel mistakes. Most assuredly, without the Ernie Cruse philosophy, I venture to say that Stage stores Inc. would not have emerged so successfully from a highly leveraged buy-out to become the great public company they are in 2013, now considered to be one of the most successful small town retailers in America.

David Slaughter

Bernard Fuchs

The final mentor that influenced me was a man named Bernard Fuchs. I first met Mr. Fuchs while he was completing a transaction bringing Palais Royal and Bealls together as he merged two smaller chains into a larger one. The first time I met Mr. Fuchs I was as an assistant manager in Lufkin, Texas. Call it luck, call it good timing, call it karma, whatever it was, meeting Mr. Fuchs and working under him was a major opportunity. He understood that Palais Royal needed capital to grow and that the Bealls chain was a gold mine worth mining.

Although many people still think that Palais Royal bought Bealls that is simply not the case. The merger was the brain—child of Bernard Fuchs. He knew that Bealls was struggling financially, organizationally and strategically. They had operated as a strong family owned business that started in East Texas that had the potential to grow and marketed as the key retailer in small town America. Mr. Fuchs was aware that Bealls owned a state of the art distribution center in Jacksonville, Texas that could handle a company two or three times the size of the Bealls. He also knew one of the reasons that Bealls was struggling was because they had not yet been able to utilize the million-dollar hardware purchased to make the distribution center work effectively. He knew they needed to learn how to use it, without bankrupting the Bealls chain in the process.

Mr. Fuchs recognized Bealls as a home-grown company and he studied the core base of stores and determined that they had never maximized "Major Opportunities" to sell career merchandise for women, better shoes and better fashion soft goods. Mr. Fuchs, in charge of Palais Royal in Houston, knew that fashion and career merchandise was their forte. Bernard Fuchs was an industry giant and true to that reputation; he created something brilliant called Stage Stores Retailers, the name at that time of the parent company. He hand pocked three Bealls Stores, Lufkin, Jasper and Nacogdoches where he would perform a six-month test while studying and completing the logistics and details of the merger.

"Major Opportunities"

He took all of the Bealls staple stock merchandise out of those three stores, transferring it to other surrounding stores that had needs and in several big shipments, he replaced the merchandise with Palais Royal goods as the three stores began to receive Palais Royal shipments as well. They had to learn, understand and operate under both companies operations and communicate with the Houston buying division at the same time, serving as test bunnies for two companies merged into one. Fortunately, I was the assistant manager in one of those stores in Lufkin, Texas. I was in the right place at the right tine but remember I turned down a promotion choosing to stay in Lufkin and inside my door of "Major Opportunities."

Mr. Fuchs had very little patience for incompetence, stupidity or for mediocrity. He quickly developed a reputation for calling people out in meetings as he spoke plainly, as one that did not miss a detail, and he was a perfectionist. On one hand, the Palais Royal executives, and district managers now had some competition and their level of protection probably reduced with that competition. On the Bealls management side, Mr. Fuchs saw potential but he expected high IQ to come with potential as part of the complete package. The rural accents and small town common sense folks from Bealls could easily get lost in translation sometimes but in the end, Mr. Fuchs understood the "Major Opportunities" of such a merger and to his credit, he judged leaders mostly on short-term results, upon potential, hard work, attitude and only then upon long-term capabilities.

Mr. Fuchs ran a tight ship and I respected him like a father. He saw the potential in me the minute we met in Lufkin and that never changed. He was masterful, he was brilliant and he was a visionary. He would continue to be an important entity in our company until it was time for him to turn the reins over to someone else. In a successful public company, it proved important to the board and to the market to demonstrate succession planning by presenting an executive plan for transition. Mr. Fuchs was wise enough and he cared deeply enough about the company to know when to allow that process to begin and then he let it run its course. When he left, the company lost a great leader; personally, I do not think we were ever the same.

I cannot adequately express the role these mentors played in my life. The difference between these men and the typical boss can be summed up in a quote I read, "The mediocre teacher tells. The good teacher explains. The superior teacher demonstrates. The great teacher inspires." All four men were great teachers. As we prepare to move into the next chapter, I want to leave you with a challenge, to make an effort to study and to apply the best from each person you work with. Find a mentor, who will teach you, become a student who wants to learn and become the teacher—a mentor, yourself.

As much as I abhor negativism, I must add as we discuss the impact of others upon our careers that one can learn something from everyone they work with. You can learn from the good, the bad and the ugly. Trust me when I say I too have seen ugly, reflected in hypocrisy, personal problems, bitterness and selfishness. These are traits to avoid duplicating since they are formulas for failure. The ugly doors are those that you shut after they leave or after you leave because they do not help you on your journey to maximize opportunities. You learn what to avoid doing, how not to treat people, on your way to the top, but you do learn from both. Avoid selecting someone as a mentor that does not follow the rules, is inconsistent in their attitude and allows personal issues to cloud their store responsibilities.

What I encourage you to do is to learn from what they all teach you and apply it as both a principle and a good habit. To be teachable, one has to want to learn, to be teachable one has to be willing to listen and to follow, to be teachable, one has to want to be taught. One has to be willing to ask questions and to learn not to make the same mistakes. Great teachers have a short patience span for someone who repeats the same mistakes repeatedly but the patience they exhibit which becomes your learning curve is worth learning. It is the right combination of knowledge and

"Major Opportunities"

experience gained from those you report to that helps develop your unique style. Mentors tend to open doors with large openings and they are willing to offer a lending hand, willing to pull you, to push you or drag you into the door.

~ Chapter 6 ~
"Major Opportunities Require Change"

Over the years, in whatever role I played at Stage Stores Inc., one of the challenges as a sales associate, a store manager, a district manager, and as an executive was how to accept, deal with, and apply changes. Many changes occurred often over my years under different management teams especially during the bankruptcy years. Not only did upper management leadership shift dramatically from time to time but also technology was always evolving which demanded we keep an open mind and demonstrate a willingness to adjust to change. As I reflect, it was clear that major opportunities often required change as part of the formula for success.

In order to deliver upon a promise I made that I would offer advice on how to avoid a path to ruin and defeat, I prefer to limit much of my time to the period between 1998 and 2000, prior to bankruptcy when things were great. I also want to talk about 2001 until 2007 when Stage Stores Inc. emerged from bankruptcy to become the successful company they are today, considered to be one of the true leaders in the industry in 2013.

The first period, 1998-2000 was a good one as the door of opportunity was wide open for everyone in the company. It was an exciting time for both companies; Palais Royal and Bealls, by now was successfully merged into one strong company called

Specialty Retailers Inc. and I had become a district manager in Houston while the company was preparing to go public down the road. Investors were extremely interested in our high potential company and the market seemed ready for the growth spurt of a company Mr. Fuchs had formed into a strong, profitable company. Mr. Fuchs was beginning to relinquish his main responsibilities as he had been preparing to turn the reins over to his replacement in training for two years, Carl Tooker, who would take the company public as his primary goal. Without beating a dead horse by ginning up negative ancient history, Stage Stores Inc. took a ride on the high side for a few years. Carl Tooker did indeed take us public which was quite an accomplishment and for a quite a while it was exciting, fun, rewarding and was truly exhilarating. We grew to fifty-six district managers during those boom years and we added high potential individuals from the outside as we seemed headed to the stars. We acquired many new stores as we grew at record pace in rural America, our forte. There appeared to be no limits to our "Major Opportunities." It would be during those two years that I would grow into an upper management status, overseeing my own district, two others and eventually, promoted to regional manager.

Growing Pains can kill Company Growth

Unfortunately, we grew excessively fast, too soon, in the wrong places, at the wrong times and in all the wrong ways. A branded company with over fifty-five years of history as Palais Royal and Bealls stores throughout Texas primarily was a company like most that thrives on comp store results from their base group of stores. As a public company with the pressures to perform each quarter, the future of the company became contingent upon steady store growth each year through the addition of new stores and acquisitions. Unfortunately, we were not prepared to find and secure enough locations or to force enough deals to grow at 20%, an expectation by the street. Therefore, the pressure to acquire other companies that were affordable or available throughout the country was unprecedented. Although I did not personally see the ice burgs floating in the cold waters as we left the warm waters of comp stores sales, I came to accept that when you go public, the pressure to grow is insurmountable. It would become those same pressures succumbed to that would inevitably take a great company down for the count, sadly, with the livelihood of many employees attached to it like one big anchor.

Due to this pressure to grow, we began to acquire companies outside our comfort zone cold weather climates. This fact complicated the buying division's margin of error and reduced the effectiveness of their decision-making, as they were outside their comfort zone of warm climate purchasing; distracted by accelerated growth as well. As was our store operations team, the buying division had great difficulty-keeping pace with company expansion plans. In order to take the company public to begin with we had repeatedly sold it as a strategy that could work in small towns throughout the country and that was simply not the truth.

As I reflect, it seems clear that the Bernard Fuchs exit was when we began to leaving warm waters (climates) and heading toward ice burgs by purchasing in northern markets almost exclusively. After all, he had successfully molded two companies into one, carefully growing the sales and merchandise content while combining best practices from each company in order to make one most efficient. He had trimmed the fat that Carl Tooker added by reapplying a leaner, trimmer volume producing company nearing 500 stores at the time he departed. Unfortunately, we were going the opposite direction now. In a time where sales were still good, morale was high, there were many new people jumping into our ship, the company was changing dramatically. In retrospect, we wasted a ton of money on things that did not add sales or profit to the bottom line. I do not think Mr. Fuchs would have let it happen.

Back to the warm water into cold heading toward ice burgs story, we would soon find out the hard way that it is a different process altogether when a company buys for cold weather stores. Although our company was adept at the southern buying-allocation process, it took too long to get ahead of the curve, satisfying the needs of several newly acquired companies in northern markets. It took too much attention from our core base of established stores, the heart and soul of the company, the "brand." We spent millions of dollars on stores acquired in other states and then we spent significant amounts of money remodeling them, adding expensive fixtures and re-merchandising stores under a name no one recognized.

    I recall a contest in the main office held to select a name for newly acquired stores in the north. Looking back on it, I should have recognized we were in trouble back then but I was on the ship too and it seemed it was safe based upon confidence in the market with our growth each quarter. "This ship had been built to withstand just about anything," I thought to myself. Sadly, we were now loaded snuggly on the titanic without enough life-boats once again and we kept picking up passengers as we never even saw the largest ice burg floating directly in front of us. Ironically, the name selected was "STAGE," and is now the parent name for the company, Stage Stores Inc. So, what's in a name you might ask? Everything and nothing as it is the "brand," that really matters. Fortunately, the brand was still there and could be re-built and the name survived because the brand grew stronger.

    In the end, we would strike that ice burg head on and it would all come crashing down and become a difficult period for Stage Stores Inc. You can do your own research on the crash of 2000 a Stage. I know there are other opinions but I was there, I was on the ship, I was a survivor, I helped rebuilt the ship, bigger and better. In the final analysis, to come back from near death as a retailer, it required a structured re-organization, meaning we had to close stores, reorganize upper management, rethink our assortments and allocation of merchandise, and re-establish credibility in the merchant world. It would result in lots of work by store personnel to survive the shipwreck. The good news is it worked and we did it, as a team. Stage Stores Inc. eventually emerged triumphantly and now offers an incredible example of a door of success that opened wide as a retailer that emerged from a 450 million dollar leveraged buy-out. It provides an example of what can happen when you maintain a focus and a commitment on the stores, when you make sound business decisions, when you learn from mistakes and finally, when you do what is right for the people in your company as the top priority, you can survive.

A ship called "Stage Stores Inc." will never sink!

I credit Jim Scarborough, the CEO, recruited by Ernie Cruse and Vivian Baker much of the credit for the complete turn-around. Ironically, he was be recruited to return to the same company that years prior he had served as chief merchandiser for back during our early Bealls days. His inspiration, his leadership, his example and his attitude set the tone for a healthy recovery. He believed we could do it and he was the stimulus for us to work together as one team. His business acumen, his experience, his passion and his love for people, would all be invaluable tools to take on this herculean task. Great leaders lead and Jim was a great leader and a wonderful human being. In the end, we were aboard a ship called Stage Stores Inc. and it was a ship that would not sink.

As the head of Human Resources for many years well prior to that crash until now, Ron Lucas also played a gigantic role in making sure the best people were maintained in our company and that great minds and assets were recruited and developed over the years to assist meeting the needs of re-building our company. He has been with Stage Stores Inc. for many years now and his team of HR personnel and staff are one of the finest retail HR teams assembled in the country from top to bottom. He is still a huge part of the Stage Stores Inc. success in 2013

My boss Ernie Cruse was also a critical link to insuring we stayed above water, righting the ship as we began to sail away from ice burgs, to sail into a vision of success and Ernie was the Captain all the way into the warm waters of recovery. For forty-eight years, he gave everything he had to this great company and he was the best leader I worked with. Besides, he promoted Pat and me to run the stores and that fact alone qualifies him as the genius I know him to be.

Having reassured you that we made things right in the end, one of the promises I made to you at the beginning is that I would share what I learned from the ordeal of bankruptcy. Going through a bankruptcy, seeing the company you love become highly leveraged, watching as a company that for fifteen long years you have poured your heart and soul into fight for their life, is not fun. In fact, it was painful to watch. I saw many changes occur during those first fifteen years prior to bankruptcy. Naturally, of course I saw a completely different set of changes post-bankruptcy. The good news for those of you reading this is bankruptcy is avoidable. Stage Stores Inc.'s record provides proof that coming out of bankruptcy is possible with the story serving as a poster child for complete recovery. Both results—one bad (bankruptcy), and one good (successful recovery), require an acceptance and adjustment to change since they both depend upon how necessary changes are implemented, accepted and applied.

In post-bankruptcy, Ernie insisted that we had to learn from our previous mistakes. During those years I served as a Sr. V.P., one of the biggest challenges was to remain open to suggestions, to be willing to consider new ways to drive sales; yet to remain cautiously wary of ideas tried and retried, those that had failed and failed again. It required patience, on-going communication with the buyers, the strength as a leader to say no, and sometimes, it required a title of Sr. V.P. Ernie encouraged us to be careful what we initiated, to be careful what we recommended and careful of the implications of each of our decisions. He reminded us that with a title of Sr. V.P., "People would jump; they would often do what we said to do without hesitation," he said. He warned us to be careful because our decisions, actions and our implemented changes could dramatically affect lives, benefits, careers, and the families of our employees. "This time," Ernie would say, "They depend on us not to screw it up, so don't screw it up boys and don't screw it up for me," I remember him saying with a serious smile one time.

I advise upper management, or for that matter, all members of management in an organization to govern with a similar thought process with a firm understanding that, "What you do has a direct impact upon others and that you better remember that with each decision you make, big or small, you will affect many people's future." You must consistently ask yourself, do the decisions I make provide long-term security for our employees or do they put them at risk? Do the changes I consider make us stronger as a company or is it just another way to do something with someone's name attached to it? In this chapter, I want to address the need for change while providing tips on how to survive changes by remaining focused upon what matters, the customers and the employees.

One of the most important things we had to embrace was what one of our store operations leaders said in a meeting when he said, "Change is good, Change is our friend." He said it in jest but he was actually correct. The world hates change, yet it is usually what brings about progress. Change will happen; it has to occur in a healthy, evolving world. Without change, where would we be? Companies, organizations, individuals that cannot change or cannot adjust to change just simply cannot survive. In a company, change is necessary, needed and be embraced. We had to embrace change and change there would be, this second time around.

A second thing that had to change was the "culture," of our company. As I mentioned earlier, we still had a great "Brand," somewhere still in the mix, however disjointed it may have been for a few years. After all, we had been in business for over sixty years in the two larger pieces of the pie, Bealls and Palais Royal. After all, Bernard Fuchs had taken two good companies and formed them into one great company prior, so we knew things could change again for the better, we just began rebuilding the ship. One of the lessons we learned coming out of bankruptcy was the need to improve consistency of store standards in order to return to a reasonable standard of clean, neat and organized as the only acceptable standard of practice. This was the Ernie Cruse way. In Hein-sight, we lost focus in the core stores with out of control growth and we had taken our eye off the ball. Those of us left at store level knew how to regain our focus instinctively bred in us over those early Bealls years. Ernie spent a lot of time in those first few years wearing many hats in his role supervising 550 stores, always keeping the employees in his sights as the most important priority, just as Jim did.

One of my most memorable recollections was the one that opened our eyes in terms of how important the "culture," of a company is. It occurred in the second year after we successfully emerged from bankruptcy. Things were looking bright as we were consistently enjoying strong sales increases, we were exceeding financial plans and we had a stable district manager team in place. Upper management had regained credibility from the streets perspective once again and now literally it seemed the sky was the limit as we were clearly going to do it all over again.

In our post-bankruptcy comfort zone, Ernie summoned Pat and me to a call after lunch one afternoon. We waited on the phone patiently, having no clue what he wanted; after all, we were on fire in sales results, perhaps he wanted to congratulate us again. Instead of discussing how well we were performing in sales this time, Ernie informed us he had gotten into his car that morning, dressed casually and that he had stopped at six of our stores on his way to Austin. No one knew he was going, including us. On the other hand, sadly, none of the stores he stopped at ever realized he was in their store. Five of the stores were mine and only one was Pat's and I recall Ernie saying something like, "You boys need to wake up." "You need to stop showing up for your little scheduled visits with the stores knowing you are coming. They work to get their store cleaned up prior to your scheduled visit, we end up spending extra payroll and then you guys tell me the stores are in great shape." He continued, as we were in no position to interrupt, "I do not want the stores to look great for you guys, I want to know they are clean, neat, and organized for the customers, day in and day out." He did not stop as he went on to say, "And you two better not start running in trying to catch them doing wrong now. Instead, you need to satisfy yourselves that our "culture," is such that we are maintaining our stores consistently every day, whether we were there or not." "It's not about catching them doing something wrong boys, it is about creating a culture of right that is consistent for all the right reasons." He never yelled at us because he knew we too cared deeply for the company and for him as well.

This was a wake-up call for both of us and would have a dramatic effect upon our entire company. However painful it was to begin going into stores unannounced, it helped us learn how to run stores that could succeed in good times or bad. We needed a new mantra it seemed. Ernie never beat us up again as he trusted us but he was willing to hold us accountable and he allowed us to take the necessary steps to change the "culture." He taught us not to over react and run the risk of crushing the morale of hard working dedicated employees that needed to share in the vision we had. Our new philosophy was actually an old philosophy, one that Ernie knew worked well. It was to maintain as the top priority, as our mantra, "stores that were clean, neat and organized," to get them the right merchandise, to spend our money as if it was theirs and to insist upon accountability from top to bottom.

Culture Change Counts for Something!

You know I like to tell stories, so let me offer one that occurred during this transition time. It is a story that had a significant impact upon store visitation within my territory. It is a story that illustrates how much culture change matters to an organization. As I began visiting with district managers and store managers concerning maintaining consistency in their store, I applied a history lesson using an analogy comparing how we had been reacting by over preparing for visits to the early American quest for independence. I compared our previous business practices to

"Major Opportunities"

Paul Revere's ride during this quest for independence when he reportedly exclaimed through the night, "The British are coming, the British are coming." We too had been guilty of sending out an alarm prior to the holy visits upper management made that was similar, but it went something like this, "The visitors are coming, the visitors are coming." A district manager would be informed of an upcoming visit by rumor, by a leak or by ordinary everyday discussion concerned planned travel by a store director or a regional manager and everyone would be placed on high alert that, "The store directors are coming, the store directors are coming." Therefore, we discovered that we had to change our company "culture," we had ourselves created. We had to replace it with a culture focused upon the one reason to exist as, "The customers are coming, the customers are coming." Our number one priority had to become welcoming our customers into our home just as you might any visitor or guest and you do not typically invite someone into your home unless it is clean, neat and organized.

Now for a funny anecdote, a funny thing happened on the way to a store visit for me. During this time, I supervised fourteen districts in my territory and the regional who reported to me handled seven of those for us. I was expected one day in San Angelo to visit one of my seven districts, at least everyone thought that was where I was going but by accident in changing planes in Dallas, through some weird set of circumstances, I got on the wrong plane and landed in Lubbock instead. When I landed, a light went off as I realized quickly it was still my territory, they did not expect me in Lubbock that day and the district manager could deliver me to the other one in between their districts, so no harm, no foul, it seemed. I called the district manager, Jeff Bailey, and asked him to come get me at the airport, 'surprise surprise!" is what I said when I called him. We visited several stores in his district with no advance notice and we experienced good, the bad and the ugly. I still believe the regional manager and district manager probably still think it was on purpose but it was really just a complete accident.

In the meantime, it sent a ripple throughout my 200 stores that "Slaughter is coming, "Slaughter is coming." I could hear the battle cry ring out from town to town, so I simply let the rumors fly while teaching a lesson that it is not about me. Poor Paul Revere, what a long ride he must have had that night since there were twenty-eight states to cover in my territory. Although the strategy we were going for was to make sure the customer was the one we prepared for, it did not hurt for the stores to be prepared every single day as best they could. As a result, our stores improved over the next 12 months in terms of becoming neater, cleaner and more organized, we had our mantra now.

Ernie's trip to Austin, that call from him while on the road and our plan of action going forward would have a permanent effect on the next four or five years, all of them were successful by the way. Please do not be naïve as we still had plenty of visits from buyers as vendors, investors and corporate personnel still visited our stores frequently. In those circumstances, you just had to accept your hypocrisy and justifiably throw out the culture change one more time by resorting to that historical message of Paul Revere, "The visitors are coming, the visitors are coming," I mean, "The British are coming, the British are coming."

Another change essential in post-bankruptcy was how to avoid a regular worst practice in a badly run company. A company, any company can find itself engaged in crisis management represented by making the same mistakes, many times in a panic mode or by rolling out change that is untested or communicated poorly. Healthy change should not come about as the result of one person saying it will work or by doing it a second time by repeating a process relying upon a flawed idea or notion that has previously failed. One of the things I recall having to learn as we adjusted to changes that were necessary to restructure our company post-bankruptcy was that we had to focus on getting it right the first time. Ernie insisted we spend quality time testing the waters by maintaining open communication with stores and store personnel from sales associates to managers to district managers. He also believed all major changes should be tested prior to being assigned to the stores to execute. Consequently, we never rolled out something new that was untested or that could not completed by a reasonable person, within a reasonable time-frame, while accomplishing the intended results.

In too many companies these days, decisions of major change trickle down from too high in the kingdom, sometimes from the kings themselves who may be unaware of the reality in the field. The term store employees use is "from the suits upstairs." In a great company, effective execution of successful change begins and ends with those who must implement the change. Our store operations team applied this philosophy in order to minimize mistakes, in an effort to improve the probability that change could happen expediently, and in order to accomplish the result we had intended. When we say, "Change is good, change is our friend," we really mean that change is intended to do something good that can improve our situation or modify it in order to improve or maximize results.

The changes we experienced in our years of recovery would often result in frustration from folks in the corporate office. The field understood that decisions made in the ivory halls of a corporate office when improperly applied do not usually end well. The ones not well thought out from a practical standpoint would often result in looks of confusion and frustration on the faces of our store management teams. As they opened their mail packet, they might think or even comment, "Really, are they that stupid, they need to get out here and see what is going on." A few times I was actually present when someone opened the mail packet and shaking their head, mumbling under their breath, would say, "Here we go again, we've already tried this, and it was a disaster, it's the same ole story." Sometimes, in my defensiveness, I would reach the conclusion that it was due to the explanation of change or that it was not well explained in a conference call with District Managers and then with the store managers but sometimes, we were just wrong. We tried to keep those of us making decisions from looking stupid yet when a mistake was made, we owned up to it.

Changes occur for many reasons but those that are well tested with the kinks ironed out in advance of a company roll out, are the ones that work well. It requires careful planning and it is critical that any changes implemented in policy or procedure is communicated effectively from the outset. If the stores cannot understand the instructions, they will not execute well and that leads to a bad change, a bad result or an unintended result. You may have had good intentions when you decided upon a change but it can easily get lost in translation, leaving the stores left scratching their heads wondering what their home office is thinking. My boss Ernie was obsessed with the main office always being perceived and functioning as a support group for the stores.

It is essential that store managers and district managers sell any changes made well to employees. Staying on the same page via weekly conference calls from the top down is very important. Worth of note for some of you that already utilize conference calls as many companies do, just because you have one each week, just because you have an agenda for one, just because you get everyone on the call that is supposed to be on there, does not automatically mean they are as effective as they can be. Allowing others to talk on a call, providing an atmosphere that causes them not to dread a conference call is important to accomplish the desired result you intend. The worst conference calls I have had were ones where I dominated the conversation and the best — the most productive ones were where everyone jumped in, where participants communicated and shared no matter how relevant the topic. It is what Ernie termed not micro-managing your subordinates. One cannot accomplish positive change by mandate it usually works best based on how you treat people in daily conversation and in on-going communication that occurs naturally through-out the year.

Test the waters before you sail around the World!

To be effective, changes have to be tested, well-communicated, implemented and tracked. Too often, companies, organizations

"Major Opportunities"

and institutions do an inadequate job of following up to determine if the intended result that justified the change, was effective or was implemented effectively. They assume it did because no one said it did not. The way to insure that it is working is to get out there and to see it in the field. My fear is that many a present day company could not tell you by having someone show you how to do, by insisting that you see it done in person, if it works the way they wrote it to work in an office environment. Only by utilizing this process can a company insure that change is good, in a way that it is our friend.

Change is good because it allows for newness necessary to improve and to remain current. Although not everyone embraces change in the manner intended. Sometimes, it calls for a unique strategy in order to maximize the way in which changes are best perceived by others. One example that comes to mind pertains to a project I undertook. It encompasses a local nail salon I have frequented over the last ten years. You will hear about Candy's Nail and Spa Salon again later when I tell you a heart-warming story involving my five year old, Ellie. In the meantime, this story is about change.

The owner of the salon for many years, Cindy, decided it was time for retirement and as the owner of a valuable piece of real estate in an expensive Houston community called Bellaire, she made the decision to rent it to another entrepreneur. Over a period of three months, the new owner made many changes. She changed lighting, re-painted, re-arranged, replaced chairs, added beautiful pictures and she created special nooks of opportunity within the same four walls that Cindy had operated over the years. Cindy's salon always looked great, she consistently maintained a top staff with loyal customers and she too had made subtle changes to keep things current and to avoid the boredom and monotony of routine.

Each time I went into the newly decorated, refurbished nail salon, the changes made the salon more appealing to the human eye as she continued to put her personal touch on the inside and outside of her establishment. I complemented her while watching suspiciously as the changes developed in a seemingly expensive manner, all the way appreciating that change is good because change is our friend. I went into get a manicure one Saturday and I noticed a hand written sign that read, "WE RESERVE THE RIGHT TO REFUSE SERVICE TO ANYONE." As the new sign was the first thing I noticed, I was curious and I asked what that sign meant. To me, a long-standing customer in newly updated salon, it stood out like a sore thumb to me. They said that they had to deal with a man off the street who stumbled in drunken one day recently and they required him to leave. Then they posted the sign, now displayed to send a very loud message that drunks will not be tolerated in this establishment.

Slightly more inquisitive, being a previous store director that exhibited great disdain for hand-made signs in any of my stores, I asked the manager in a semi quiet tone, "Who is that sign was for, the drunks or the customers?" She said, "We will not tolerate drunks," we care about our customers." I proceeded to put on my "Trainer Dave" hat and as her attention turned to me, I opened a door of opportunity called a teaching session and they began to listen more attentively now. Aware that I knew the answer to the question I had posed, I continued my lesson and I said, "So, will you run every drunk out of Candy's nails if they come in and cause a scene like that"? The answer was, "Yes." I went on, "Well then what message do you really want to send to your customers with that sign prominently displayed in this salon?" I continued, "Do you want them to think you have a huge problem with drunks that are wandering in? The answer was, "No." Then I said, "Do you have a big problem with these drunks coming in on a regular basis." "No, not very often," the manager admitted.

"Trainer Dave" proceeded to coach them about the effective use of signing and about customer service. I said, "If it was me, I would take that sign down right now, and I might put up a sign that promotes the positive changes you have made for your customer, the very same customers you said matter the most to you." The owner whispered in my ear that she had spent over $60,000 on improvements in three months, implying that

"Major Opportunities"

her investment was huge, reflecting that she was hopeful for a payback very soon. Out of a sense of commitment to the salon that I love and out of dedication to promoting changes with sound business advice, even possibly out of guilt for opening my mouth, I said, "What if we put up a professional sign, one that reflects why you made changes. I offered, "Why don't I work on some ideas with you and I will have a sign made that we can put up for all of your customers to see, free of charge, as my gift to you?" They nodded and smiled at me, indicating approval and support and suddenly it appeared we were now on the same team.

I designed four versions of the sign and the owner and I agreed on which of the four options was best suited for the salon. I selected a local company to print the sign professionally and I framed it in a sleek black twelve by eighteen frame and. I delivered it to them the week after Christmas. I helped place the sign on a prominent wall as the new owner indicated I could put it anywhere I wanted. I completed my training exercise by recommending they keep a close watch out for customers whose eyes might wander to the sign and I added that they should listen when someone made a comment about the framed addition to their salon. I reminded them that they should use every major opportunity with the sign serving as a silent reminder that "Change is good, change is our friend," therefore, Candy's Nail Salon, is our friend. I coached once again when I concluded, "Let's use that sign to reflect positively upon the wonderful changes that have been made." Then, of course, I got my manicure. The manager refused to charge me for my manicure and I accepted her courtesy this one time only. I told her that I was not out to get things for free, that all I wanted to do was to practice what I preach and truly in my mind, I wanted to practice what I write.

Sometimes, changes implemented are not fully utilized as the vehicle for promoting the change as well as they could be. I ask you, which sign has a better chance of helping the owners changes improve the customer base of the salon, the one saying, "We reserve the right to refuse to serve you" or the one that reflects we spent $60,000 on changes for YOU? You are correct; the professionally made sign saying we did it for you because we care is the one that is best! It offers an opportunity for Candy's doors to be open for many more years by appreciating customers that come in. Interestingly, I returned many more times for manicures since that holiday season and each time I am told more customers comment about the new sign, and each time I leave knowing that most of the time the slogan is right, "Change is good, change is our friend."

CANDY'S
Nails Spa & Facial

WE MADE SOME CHANGES
BECAUSE WE CARE, FOR YOU!

Photo provided by the author

~ Chapter 7 ~

"In Tragedy or Crisis-Major Opportunities May Arise!"

As I researched materials for this book I met many interesting people each with a unique, almost always inspirational personal story to describe life's ups and down's in their search to achieve happiness, contentment and success. I visited with some who have had to deal with personal tragedy as I have yet they too were able to find the strength to meet future opportunities, perhaps in some way to redeem them-selves as well. It is possible they too were seeking some relieve from a deep, hidden pain, from within them. The strength, power, determination and courage of those I interviewed helped me confirm that I am not the only one out there with a painful secret and that I am not the only one who has experienced a crisis of human tragedy. I knew when I began to write this book that my personal story, as painful as it might be to recount and to record was one I needed to share. I felt it was important for you to know that even when tragedy or crisis occurs, "Major Opportunities," may arise.

David Slaughter

An Early Tragedy: The Reese Dennis Story

This first story is one that will always stick with me. Although this tragedy did not pertain to me personally, it affected me deeply and it caused me to choose a path that would open all the doors in my life that really mattered. It is a story about the influence one person can have upon another. This story is about a young man named Reese Dennis. Reese and I attended the same church in Houston called West University Church of Christ. Reese was three years older than I was. He was one of the most talented, gifted young men I have ever met in my lifetime. He was years ahead of all of us in maturity. I can recall hearing Reese preach in front of 10,000 teenagers at the Sam Houston Coliseum at a Houston Youth Lectureship back in 1971. Reese was only about five foot five as I recall and that day they put an empty coke box in front of the podium so that he could reach the microphone. Although I can no longer remember exactly what he said that day, I do remember how motivating and inspiring he was to the crowd and I remember that he looked ten feet tall from way out in the audience.

Reese was a debater at Lamar High School. He was a senior and I was a freshman at Bellaire High School. I knew he was a very good high school debater. I also knew he traveled as the top team at his high school and that he competed accordingly. I only signed up for debate at Bellaire because I knew Reese debated and if he did it, it must be an important thing to do. I recall how Reese made me feel, how he treated me as a person. My first year at Bellaire High School they called us baby debaters. One of the tournaments we attended was at Lamar High School. Reese was President of the debate team at Lamar and as it turns out one of Reese's responsibilities during the first day of the tournament was to take his turn selling drinks in their concession area. I was with some of my other Bellaire "baby debaters" and we decided to go and get a soft drink. I saw Reese from a distance and told the others, "That guy is Reese Dennis," and I added, "He and I are friends you know." They scoffed and remarked, "You moron, you

"Major Opportunities"

don't know Reese Dennis, he's Lamar's top debater, he doesn't even know who you are, he is a senior, stupid." "Really," I said, "Let's just go see about that."

Anxiously and somewhat cautiously, I walked towards Reese with my friends. Before we even got up there Reese said loudly to me, "David, man it's great to see you, I bet your going to win it all for Bellaire, aren't you tiger." I was beaming as soon as he spoke and now they were picking their mouths back up off the floor when he addressed only me for the second time, "What ya have, Dave?" He made me feel so special that I knew him, although I barely did. I got ready to pay for my coke and in front of my fellow Bellaire debaters he said, "No way man, I got you covered." There was one more gasp from the peanut gallery. It seems I really was a stud all of the sudden to the other little "baby debaters." As we walked away I turned back to give him a glance that said, "Thank you," and I saw something that defined Reese Dennis to the as he took a dime out of his own pocket and paid for my drink, he put the money in the till for me. Reese did not just preach to 10,000 of Houston's youth that you should be honest, genuine, and sincere, he lived that way each day, something that would stay with me forever. He did not just give me that drink on the house; he paid for it out of his own pocket. For you see, Reese chose to live the same way in both of his worlds, in church and in the real world. To me, he defined that day the deeper meaning of the kind of light we can be in the world, one that reflects truth, integrity and faith.

That year Reese went on the win the Texas State debate tournament, automatically qualifying him for the national debate tournament held only a few months later. Sadly, before Reese could attend that highly honored tournament, a terrible tragedy occurred. One Wednesday night services were interrupted as one of the church leaders went up to address the crowd. Slowly, choking back tears, reluctantly as if he hoped it was not real, he informed the congregation that Reese Dennis had slipped, fallen in the shower and died. Reese was an epileptic and had suffered a seizure, which resulted in the fall, a blow to his head and his tragic death.

Shock and grief followed quickly and as I sat there that night in the audience at sixteen years old, stunned completely, choking back my tears, I made one decision that night that would completely change my life, forever. I decided right then in that church pew that no matter what I was going to become the best debater I could possibly be. No one knew, I did not tell a soul, but I decided to win, until I reached the top, I decided to win for the rest of my life. I made the decision that night to quite baseball, basketball and to put everything I had into debate. I went from playing as a "baby debater," to someone that wanted two years at Bellaire High School, one of the debate schools in the nation.

Reese would not be going to the National Debate Tournament. Sadly, the trophy he won at state would be displayed at his funeral and be buried with him forever. Reese would be gone, but not forgotten. I would go on to become a good debater in high school but in college, I would become a national circuit debater and I would receive a full scholarship for three years at HBU. Ranked as one of the top teams in the nation, we traveled for three years to the top tournaments in the nation. Although I received lots of encouragement from my grandmother and my mom, Reese was ultimately the inspiration for it. I did it for me, I did it for him and I did it for what he did not get to do. I do vividly recall in one of the most important debate rounds in college with the pressure of 800 people watching that round, stopping before I stood up to give an important speech, thinking of Reese and saying to myself, "This one is for you Reese." It was the best speech I ever delivered and I believe Reese was watching it happen. We came in first place out of 160 of the best debate teams in the nation that tournament in Tucson, Arizona.

Although my retail career was not really ever about debate, the training I received from a competitive debate experience over eight years helped me significantly. I remember pondering the squandered opportunities in college, thinking to myself that if I could beat all of those teams in debate I could accomplish anything I wanted to. It aided me along the way as I relied heavily upon a competitive nature instilled in me as I competed against the best sales persons on the sales floor with Bealls.

Even in my journey at UHD to seek the highest GPA I could in my two years from 2011-2013, it was that same burning desire to be the best that Reese had instilled in me twenty-five years prior, it was a fire that burns even to this day. I still think of Reese from time to time, I thought of him right before I delivered my commencement speech in May in front of 18,000 people. I think of the impact he had upon my life and to this day I still insist that one person like Reese can influence another so very dramatically. Sadly, his tragedy became an inspiration for me to become the best I could be. Because of Reese's tragic death, as is the case often in life, when tragedy or crisis occurs, opportunities may arise.

My Personal Tragedy

The second story I will share is of my own difficult tragedy and in the process, I will provide an example for you of how an opportunity arose for me as a result. Once upon a time, there was a great Houston debater; a person who eventually ran out of debate scholarship at an expensive school in Houston, Texas called Houston Baptist University. This person had not exactly applied himself academically. Instead, he had often put his ego first into a selfish pursuit of trophies, fame and personal recognition beating people in cross-examination debate like it was what mattered in life. He was, from an academic stand-point an under-achiever. This ex-debater often fed his insatiable, competitive drive by prepping for national debate tournaments in college, by traveling all across the nation, by competing against the best teams in the nation until there was no more money left in the scholarship fund and no one left to beat. Finally forced to reconcile the fact that he must join the real world like everyone else, he found a job and began to work part time as he pondered, reflected, even agonized upon what life would be like after eight years of debate was no more and that there was no degree in the land to be had.

A day I will not forget

On December 23, 1982 at the age of twenty-five, I was in route to a part time job at six am in the morning. I was driving my MG Midget; it was cold, icy, rainy and dark. As I turned my car to head left on Newcastle off Beechnut in Bellaire, Texas, two streets from where I grew up and my parents still lived, a terrible life-changing event happened. I never even saw him. He was walking on the right side of the street possibly taking his early morning walk. The seventy-four year old man was wearing a dark green jumpsuit and he was walking slightly in the road on my side headed the direction of my vehicle. I never saw him, but I hit him head on. I felt a very hard thump that shattered the glass panel on the right side of my front window. What had I hit? It felt like a large rock that sadly, turned out to be a human head. I pulled over in a total panic, jumped out into the icy cold rain and looking back lying on his back in the middle of the road, was the man I killed that morning. I was in shock almost immediately. I know I ran back there to check on him but over the years, I was able to block out most of that memory until forced to face my fear years later.

A sweet, seemingly faceless woman stopped to help. In full-fledged shock by now, I began running towards Beechnut to call someone from a pay phone at the local Corner Pantry, as we needed help. I ran to the same Corner Pantry I had ridden my bike to many times over the years as a kid, the same Corner Pantry where that crazy eccentric cat woman who never mowed her yard backed over my bicycle and then offered up that I could come and try and find a replacement wheel out of her junkyard. Really? That is not going to be a great explanation to my Dad, I thought. However, right now, my thoughts were not on that silly bike as I got to the pay phone, out of breath and still in shock. I called three people, the police, my Dad and my fiancé. I remember saying to my dad on the phone. "Dad, you have to come quickly, I think I just killed someone." I woke my fiancé up and I think I just said, "Please help me, I am in trouble."

I ran back to the scene of my crime, this time understanding from the view of his lifeless body with the morning light coming up on the horizon ever so slowly that there was nothing we could do as his life had left his body. Seconds lasted minutes, minutes lasted hours and that sweet little faceless woman who stopped now hugged me, held me, and loved me, as any mother would do with her own little crying child as we waited together in the cold rain for someone to come. "Please come soon, I thought to myself."

The police arrived at just about the same time as my Dad did, as I recall. I got in my Dad's car to get out of the bitter cold and the realization of what it feels like to take a human life began to hit me harder and harder by the minute. The slight warmth of his car provided little comfort to me but my Dad was as comforting as a father could be. He was not a man of real outward emotion but I remember feeling closeness with him that morning that I have not felt since. The police man came back to our vehicle twice to check on us, the officer was understandably cold, time seemed to stop as the seventy four year old father-grand-father, lay silently on his back, alone and bleeding, now frozen in the position my vehicle had thrown him. Eventually the police came back to our car and indicated that we needed to go to the police station in Bellaire and wait for them to wrap up their field report, that there was paper work to fill out when they arrived.

The police-man at the scene assured me that he could see that it was an accident almost immediately just by the location of my vehicle and from the final location of that lifeless body in the road. He tried as best he could to console me as he tried to help me understand that it was just a horrible unplanned tragedy, he said that he knew how it felt. Although he would explain that statement to me later which was comforting only slightly, it was all inconsequential to that lost life lying on a cold concrete pavement, a life I had taken. "You have to get the car home," he said to my Dad. My Dad drove me to his house where a loving Christian mother was waiting, fearing the worst as she prepared to embrace her beloved son, now making every effort to take some of the pain from his limp frail body, into her own. No words could change my harsh reality, but it is a moment where a son needs his mom and dad and they were there for me as they always have been. My precious little daddy walked back over those two streets in the cold; he drove my broken vehicle with signs of a man's head smashing into a hard glass, present in the front seat.

We headed silently to the police station in Bellaire bur I barely remember much of that at all. That is what shock will do for you, as it seems that a state of shock seeks to protect you in some way from a complete and total breakdown in a crisis of that magnitude. I sat there in the police station in a fog next to the library I had completed debate research many times over the years. I sat there next to the ballpark I had played many baseball games at, feeling as guilty as a criminal that had taken a life should feel. It took over two hours for the police to get back to the station. Those two hours passed like two days. I could hear my heart pounding, I could feel my blood pumping, my head felt like it might explode and my body was numb all over.

Finally, the police officer returned and he politely summoned us back to a private office. The frozen officer apologized profusely for taking so long as he explained that they literally had to go house to house, door to door, to determine where the man lived since he had no identification on him. Sadly, the officer reported to us that the man lived in the house that was catty corner to where my parents had lived for twenty years meaning, they were neighbors. So, my vehicle had been moved by my father from the scene was now sitting squarely in front of our house in full view of his own home, it was a car I would never set foot in again.

As the Christian father and man my Dad is, his first thought was that we should go talk to his family immediately, somehow making an effort to express our sorrow and sadness, perhaps to find a way to offer condolences for this tragedy, for this terrible, unplanned accident. The police officer interrupted my Dad, politely suggesting we avoid doing that. He said that when they went in the house there were guns laying everywhere with posters, suggesting, "An eye for an eye and a tooth for a tooth." He said in his professional opinion it was best to leave it alone. There was silence as it all continued to sink in, deeper and deeper.

Then the kind police officer told me a story that I have to share with you because in some small way it validates that in "Tragedy or crisis, opportunities may arise," and it was now his opportunity that had arisen. He looked me square in my eyes and he said to me that when he indicated at the scene of the accident that he knew how I felt, he meant he KNEW how I felt. He informed me that early in his police career he accidently hit a man out in the road. He said, like your accident today I never even saw him; he should not have been out on that stupid road but he was and I too hit and killed a man, many years ago. He told me he could not and would not lie to me by telling me I would ever be able to forget this incident. Instead, he asked me to try and understand someday soon that bad things do happen to good people, that accidents happen but that God sees everything and that he (God) knows, I did not mean to hit him. Honestly, at the time this was not very consoling to me but in the days, weeks, months and years to follow flashbacks of that conversation would provide some slight feeling of comfort as it served to validate that it was just simply an accident, that is was not my fault and I did not mean to do it.

Now I know some of you have had terrible things happen to you as well or perhaps to someone you love or to someone you care deeply about. My story is certainly not the only tragedy that someone has survived. I was fortunate in the sense that I had a loving family and a wonderful fiancé to stick by my side, to shower me with love and offer unconditional forgiveness. I cannot speak for others that have experienced such a tragedy, but I did not lose my mind and I managed to stay in the game of life. I suspect that the values and character that my parents had instilled in me so early on managed to protect my mind somehow from imploding but it was my heart and my soul that needed mending and that might take years.

David Slaughter

One cold morning in Montana

Perhaps now you are left wondering how such a terrible human tragedy could become an opportunity for me down the road. Well that requires another story, sadly, another tragedy. Years later as a regional manager I was assigned to the Montana region and I was traveling with one of my district managers, Tari Wells. We were on a Montana highway in route to one of her Saturday store meetings. Coincidently it was again freezing cold; and it was about eight am in the morning. As we drove along a long stretch of barren high-way we were the very first vehicle to come upon a very bad accident. A car had just left the road and was flipping through a field within our line of sight. Tari stopped her vehicle and without her ever knowing what was going through my mind, within seconds, my mind went back to that horrible tragedy in Bellaire, Texas. Consequently, I had to face my fear as I recollected seeing the seventy-four year old man vividly in my head once again, as he lay dying in the street. Tari was pregnant, I had no choice and there was no time to waste. I had to get out if that vehicle right then, step into the cold blistering Montana wind by myself and do what I could do to help. I suspected it was not pretty but I did not hesitate for a moment, as it was my time to minister, it was now time to face my fear, my opportunity had arisen.

As it turns out an aunt and her niece had been driving for a very long distance all night. The aunt had pulled over as she was exhausted and gave the wheel to drive to the niece while she slept for a while. Sadly, her little niece was only eleven years old and when I got out in the Montana field she was understandability in complete hysterics and shock. The aunt, thrown wildly from the vehicle into the field, was thrashing about but at least she was moving some and still breathing. All I could do was hold, love, and try to console that precious little eleven year old in the same fashion as that sweet, faceless little woman had done with this twenty five year old grown man some fifteen years prior. I faced my fear with great certainty, I got myself out of that car because I

"Major Opportunities"

was needed right then. I was indeed, part of the master plan that day.

Fortunately, the second car that stopped contained a nurse and she knew not to move the aunt, "An ambulance was in route," she stated. As more and more cars stopped I was no longer needed. As I climbed back into Tari's car I did not break down as you might think but I was compelled to tell Tari of the fear that I had just been forced to face head on. Tari was supportive and she is one of the most wonderful people I have ever met. As we drove quietly the rest of the way to her store meeting, I reflected silently in my head. I now understood that in facing my fear the opportunity had arisen for me to help in some tiny seemingly insignificant way, just by being there to be there. By consoling that eleven-year old, if for only a moment while she watched her aunt lay dying in that cold empty Montana field. Sadly, we read in the newspaper that next day that the aunt had died from massive internal injuries. While I had been holding her niece's little hand, her head on my chest, crying her eyes out, her aunt lay dying, helpless and alone.

I do still pray for that young girl from time to time privately; she is some twenty-six years old by now. My prayer for her has always been that she too has recognized and accepted that it was only an accident, a terrible unplanned tragedy and my prayer for her is that she too may somehow, someday be of comfort to another in a moment of tragedy or crisis, as she and I have experienced. I pray that she might have the strength over time to rise above the guilt and the pain she feels each year on that day and be able to replace that pain with goodness, love and mercy, all the days of her life. Occasionally, my mind will drift back to that moment in time, and I hope today that she is whole.

I still think of that terrible accident on December 23 each year. It does not cause me to stay in bed or to drink (I do not drink anyway); it does not send me into a spiral of deep depression. I will admit that a few years ago when we moved back into Bellaire, I found myself dropping off a flower in the exact spot where I know the tragedy occurred. No one knew I observed ritual until now for those few years as it was my private moment with God.

I think I was probably searching for some feeling of inner peace and reassurance. There is now a walk or bike path along that spot where our lives met so tragically, so many years ago. I postured even for just those three years as I placed a flower in that exact spot, perhaps the man I hit knew I was there, perhaps God was reminded, I am so very sorry, it was an accident, I did not mean to do it. I have tried to live my life, as imperfect as I am each day as an opportunity to try and do more for others by being involved in good work when I have an opportunity.

Mostly, I have tried to be as empathetic as I can be to another's pains that often seem to go unnoticed to most. I can usually recognize the pain in their eyes but I often remind myself, there is a master plan and that no matter what plan unfolds for me, I can do what I can do to give back to the world, hopefully for all of us. I know that if not for the tragedy that befell me at twenty-five, I wouldn't have been able to comfort that eleven-year-old as I did, to truly feel her pain and like my mom, making every effort to take some of the hurt and pain from her limp, frail body, into mine. I truly recognize that if I hadn't faced my fears on that cold Montana morning, my real fear is that I wouldn't have been able to jump to the aid of that postal worker in Houston years later that I described earlier in the book. So sometimes, when tragedy occurs, opportunities may arise.

What I discovered over all these December 23rds since that cold morning is that my life has meaning, my life has been fruitful and that my time on this earth has great value. I truly hope that my painful but true story helps even just one of you that may be carrying a pain or a burden as this, truly a burden that no one perhaps you and I can understand as well. I want you to realize and to accept that you can be whole, knowing that the good things you try and do every day even in the smallest of ways can go a long way towards some small act of redemption or perhaps a feeling of absolution. Doors that open are not always the ones we want to open or that we see but even painful doors can present an opportunity someday, if only to be there when you are needed by another in a crisis.

~ Chapter 8 ~
Brainstorming 101: "Finding Opportunities"

There are many resources on the market that claim to offer a formula for guaranteed success in the business world. The truth is no magic potion will guarantee future successes. What I can tell you is that not all of the advice in the world can replace good advice based upon doing it. What I can tell is this: success starts by getting your creative ideas on paper so you can see for yourself that you are smarter than you think. I prefer to rely upon a strategy that I refer to as "Brainstorming 101," one that I learned many years ago in high school, in Houston, Texas. Brainstorming, as you will learn, can turn theories into ideas—into workable ideas, the kind you need to implement in every facet of your business, the ones that help you maximize your, "Major Opportunities."

I was fortunate to attend Bellaire High School from 1973 to 1976, where I was on the debate team for all three years. Back then, Bellaire High School was ranked in the top ten academically in the state of Texas and one of the cornerstones of that ranking was the reputation of its forensic program and in particular, its debate team. Ranked as one of the nation's best programs, unlike other High Schools that might have two or three debate teams, Bellaire High School usually had sixty debate teams on our squad. In a recent conversation with the Bellaire coach, Jay Stubbs, he indicated he now has over two hundred in his program including all of the students involved in competitive speaking events.

Our debate coach Mr. David Johnson, was brilliant. He had participated in the finals of the national debate tournament in his own college days and he was adept at providing an intellectual, often sarcastic, sounding board for bright minds to operate. As it turns out, over his tenure as the coach of the Bellaire debate squad he coached, mentored, and developed literally thousands of students, who over the next few decades would become some of the most successful men and women in the country; certainly leaders among all others. They became legislators, lawyers, doctors, writers, professors, President's, Vice-Presidents, and CEO's, CFO's, and Sr. V.P.'s, successful businessmen and women alike. Many Johnson disciples became leaders in both their communities and in business.

As I reflect upon that stressful high school experience and upon his leadership, I truly believe we all owe him a great debt of gratitude for you see he expected, demanded, insisted that we act like the best, think like the best, study like the best, and perform as the best. He taught us each to carry ourselves proudly into life with a confidence that was sure to achieve results at the highest level for many of us. The competitive fire that he lit within us was one that I often relied upon in my path from sales associate without a degree to, become a senior vice president of a large public company.

I ran into one of the ex-Bellaire debaters at a Texans football game several years ago and we enjoyed a nice conversation reminiscing about the vast examples of ex-Johnson disciples that had gone on to lead in the world they live in. It reiterated to me once again the greatness of that high school experience and it reminded me that the exposure one has at an early age to even one such demanding individual, can have such a lasting impact on one's future successes. The power of positive influence from just one person is staggering. One of my hopes in writing this book is that you will become this individual for others. Your single influence, as was David Johnson's individual influence upon his debaters, can be astonishing.

Having said all of that, I must admit, we were scared to death of David Johnson much of the time. His bite was actually much worse than his bark and the bark would bite you in the butt so that you could not be comfortable in a sitting position until your sense of pride could return usually days later. We generally referred to that period as the long weekend. Back then, it was still ok to smoke in the debate shack, and smoke he did. I do not exaggerate when I say, tension often filled that smoke filled room at Bellaire High in those secluded encamped debate shacks as we were interrogated and excoriated by Johnson about the arguments we could and could not prove. Often, we were left feeling numb from our realization of stupidity and incompetence. All too often, the discussions deteriorated into a verbal lashing on any one of us for any number of reasons, usually completely justified. We might be unprepared; we might not be contributing to the conversation as we should, we might be drifting into thoughts of the next tournament we were traveling to, at the expense of receiving a harsh verbal beating for losing focus. His eyes were definitely piercing, his tongue was always sharp, and thankfully, he did not accept giving anything but the best you had to offer. His wit disguised as sarcasm is still vivid in my mind, even today.

Every day the expectation was extremely high as there were no play days in debate class, it was business as usual always, and we practiced as if we were playing the game that very day. If he sensed you were weak yet over-confident, he made it his personal job to help you come to the realization that the smartness you had as a smug, smiling, Bellaire debater paled in comparison to the reality of your confused, misinterpretation of your incompetence or an inability to fathom the deeper meaning of life.

On the other hand, fortunately, David Johnson only knew one level of success and effort and it was excellent and unadulterated. There was no room for mediocrity in his world of thought. I know many of us baby debaters, (as we were called in tenth grade) did not completely understand his methods, his approach, perhaps even sometimes his madness, he was on a constant intellectual mission to stretch our minds as far as he could and then, farther. Whether we understood his strategy then or whether it was years later when a light went off, his unique approach was unparalleled in the forensic world of high school debate. His style and pursuit of excellence caused his teaching style, his coaching style to become legendary among top academic schools in the nation. What stands out about Johnson that is distinguishing from college athletics and from other debate programs was his expectation of your success in the competitive world of debate was equally matched by the expectation that grades would be attained with the same level of excellence? Good grades were never mutually exclusive to great debate results and school trophies in David Johnson's book of success, were stacked upon books.

Incidentally, his wife who was initially the debate coach at Westchester High School, a rival debate school, went on the serve on the HISD school board and ironically, she handed my son's diploma to him as he crossed the stage for graduation at Bellaire High School in 2006. I know she did not know he was my blood, but I admired her from a distance, understanding her own dedication to greatness and of course, admiring her for putting up with Johnson, it could not have always been fun, no offense David.

Now, to elaborate on the reasons for our successes at Bellaire and to explain how this process of brainstorming can translate into your world as a tool to achieve success, for that matter, how it can help any individual in any process that requires a deliberate approach, allow me to explain. The process that David Johnson used at Bellaire High was, "Brainstorming 101." In our high school world, this translated into using our quantitative resources in order to maximize qualitative results. This process usually began with a decision by some of the senior debaters and Johnson that it was time to break out a new affirmative case as a squad. As we traveled to debate tournaments, we would be required to debate one national topic for the entire year. We would compete in four or six preliminary rounds each tournament, the teams with the best records advancing to elimination rounds, with a goal of proceeding to the finals in novice debate, standard debate and cross-examination debate formats. Of those preliminary rounds, half the time we were compelled to argue on the affirmative on behalf of change, justifying the need for change (we call that in the real world submitting legislation or a bill with some reason) and defending that the solution could be argued to be better than worse, in the final analysis.

As an affirmative team, we were fighting off a negative teams list of reasons not to make a change and to make every effort to fight off their predictions of gloom, doom and destruction that might occur because of any change to the status quo, called disadvantages. It required tons of library research even to prepare a stock affirmative case. Unfortunately, after one or two tournaments of using the same affirmative debate case as schools knew the details of what case you were running so they could become better prepared at arguing against your case as time passed, decreasing the odds you might win. One had to try to stay ahead of the curve of their argument and responses in order to continue to win on the affirmative from competition to competition.

Having explained the debate preparation process, Bellaire High School was unique in the sense that because we had so many debate teams, we had the resources to quickly change gears and roll out a brand new affirmative case on any given weekend. The surprise this afforded our school was stunning to the competition. Bellaire sent teams to three or four tournaments at a time in a given weekend to compete and this process of springing a new case on our adversaries, rumored to have caused many a nightmare for members of opposing teams, to the point of tears, often nausea, perhaps even occasionally bordering on a nervous breakdown, in some cases. It was domination of the mind and it was truly exciting. We won most often based upon our research, our preparation, and our hard work but sometimes we won, just because we were Bellaire and I bet they still do. There were other rounds with other teams, perhaps they might win one later in the tournament was our Johnson philosophy, as it became a Bellaire standard of fairness as applied to a measure of success.

The break out of a new affirmative debate case by Bellaire occurred as a direct result of coming up the with the best of the very best ideas detailed, exhaustive, extensive brainstorming sessions followed by a complete briefing of all arguments and responses to all opposing arguments that an unprepared or semi prepared team could muster. The net result in any given weekend would be that our school won almost every affirmative round we argued and often it resulted in complete sweeps of tournaments, meaning many trophies. It resulted in the opposing schools having to go back to the drawing board, headed home left scratching their heads in frustration.

As I explored the metaphorical doors of opportunity during the process of writing this book, I occasionally found myself reaching out to those who had played a huge role in my life and David Johnson came to mind. I was compelled to find him, to thank him for all of us. As I began my search I found articles by ex-debaters explaining how he had influenced them, what they had gained from him and how he had influenced them to the core. As I dug deeply into the Bellaire website I found postings validating the exact same thing, he changed our lives and we all know it, just as if Jay Stubbs is changing lives at Bellaire, even now. David Johnson is considered one of the top debate coaches of the century. The truth is David is a humble man who does not particularly like the spotlight but has always enjoyed watching his students grow, develop and succeed at the highest levels.

I emailed David after having had no contact with him for many years. I told him I was in the process of completing a book and that I debated for him back in 1973-1976, hoping that he still remembered me. His response was very Johnsonian. I could see him smiling, almost smirking as he politely responded to me, "That it amuses him that ex-debaters often wonder if he remembers them, that he remembers all of them." Of course he does, silly me, I had to know that when I sent that first email to him, some things just never change. No matter what, David

Johnson provides a great example of how one person can affect the lives of many others. His dedication to the expansion of the minds of students, to the highest standards of excellence as a top priority and his commitment to academic results with competitive achievement endear him to all of us ex-Bellaire debaters.

I requested a quote from David pertaining to debate, about the process of debate. He responded with the following email, "I really believe debate is the best game in town. Nothing really is as intensive an exercise in thinking about multiple problems. I think the real value of debate-the extension of argument, forcing depth and discussion until one side really has to say, "Uncle," is the clear value of debate. Eventually, the extension of argument exposes the charlatan, reveals the one-dimensional thinker and defuses the fanatic with one idea filling the entire skull." He continued, "If anyone doubted the power of extended argument, you only need look at the presidential debates where every time they call them "debates" their handlers are making sure there is really none of that-debate that is—but the usual one-dimensional platitudes. Add to that the cross-examination style of debate and you get a purer pursuit towards truth. Good for the court room but steadily avoided in the "presidential debates." Debate is the best device for truth and discovery, frowned upon by those running presidential campaigns." (David Johnson, December 30, 2012).

Having filled you in on my debate experiences under David Johnson, worthy of note, I decided in the process of completing this chapter to reach out to my alma mater, Bellaire, once again as a part of a research project I was working on to present to the Kettering Foundation. I contacted the coach at Bellaire now, Jay Stubbs. Jay has been at Bellaire as the coach now since 1999. He worked with David Johnson for the last several years as he was wrapping up his long-standing career at Bellaire High. Jay has coached forensic debate now for twenty-eight years himself. As we visited, I asked him for his take on how debate shapes students as they head out into the real world these days. He indicated that the most rewarding part of his job is that he is blessed with so many great students, and his greatest joy is not necessarily winning every round, but instead, as he watches his students go on to bigger and better things in life. He provided an example of one of his students listed high on the Forbes List of "30 under 30." Jay said he views coaching as, "Merely an opportunity to work with great minds, with great high potential students as they begin to move towards their potential in whatever field they choose." I had a feeling when I left that morning that another door had opened for both of us.

The process of brainstorming 101 at Bellaire High School was actually very simple. First, all of us debaters were required to be there for the entire exercise. The only excuse considered legitimate included; serious plague or disease, death of a family member that could be verified, or perhaps a hospital stay might work which of course, required a doctor's excuse. We would begin by writing all of our ideas on chalk-boards all around the debate shack. We took turns writing as our arms, hands and minds would eventually fatigue under the strain. Years later, when applied to my company, this process would require the use of flip charts with lots of markers. At a Bellaire brainstorming, any idea we could think had to be blurted out without the slightest hesitation, no idea was considered stupid and none would be rejected at first glance. The process was inclusive of everyone in the room. Frankly, it was incumbent upon each of us to speak up or we might suffer the wrath of Johnson, sort of like the wrath of Khan, so to speak. I recall finally one time saying something stupid out of panic like, "We can prove ducks quack," and upon blurting out that ignorant half-sentence, I received a look from Johnson that would cause any duck not to quack for fear of plucking.

By the end a typical two to three hour session, we left to go back out into the world to think of more ideas, to go to the library and to begin researching what could be proven. We had team leaders that consisted of seniors, juniors, and we the baby debaters just quacked right along behind them. Over the next few days this process would continue, each time becoming slightly more intense, more intimidating; yet more productive towards achieving the final result we were aiming for, to win. Within two weeks we were no longer debating amongst ourselves about the generalities of an argument, we had found the proof we were looking for and more importantly, we had responses prepared to answer all questions that might come up, we had now assembled a brand new affirmative case. The juniors and seniors prepared detailed briefs on colored paper placed neatly in acetates in new binders and we tenth graders performed the grunt work like copying. We were all part of the process of planning, preparation and assembling and we all benefited from the final product. It created a sense of pride as we left in cars and busses for tournaments, all keeping the secret of our new found weapon that was soon to be unleashed upon the forensic world as a weapon of mass destruction in our world of reasoning by cross examination.

Some years later this same simple exercise often served useful in daily business practice and became invaluable to me over time as a store manager, a district manager, a regional manager and finally as an executive within Stage Stores Inc. This all inclusive, intellectual pursuit, seeking the most desirable plan and outcome proved to be a catalyst for creativity, continuity and accomplishment throughout the twenty-four years I was involved with Stage Stores Inc. It generally always started big and ended small with a big focus, just as if it did in the Bellaire debate shacks. As details filled in the vision grew and it became one vision, our vision. I watched as my boss Ernie Cruse utilized this same exercise in weekly staff meetings. This open, candid discussion and an insistence to contribute to the conversation usually always ended with a decision that was most beneficial to our 12,000 employees and most importantly, to our customers.

I watched at our semi-annual district manager meetings written and planned by my counter-part and I became meetings that our district managers took part in planning and executing. through effective brainstorming sessions The ownership taken by our district managers in this process as we brainstormed how to apply best practices to a chain of 600 clothing stores was fun to watch unfold. It usually could be traced back to an effective brainstorming activity, followed by another and then another. The extent to which they were encouraged, challenged, even coaxed to participate had a direct measurable impact upon the successes we experienced in the field.

What I understand over those years in retail was how valuable and how practical this brainstorming process would be as a tool to improve my ability to lead, to provide direction, to make the right decisions, to include others in the vision I had, and to consistently achieve results at the highest of levels in each position I held. This process of brainstorming is one that applies to debate as I first learned it but in the real world, it applies equally well to the planning and execution of sales results, to writing training and recognition programs, to setting and enforcing standards of performance within any business, company or organization.

You too can benefit from brainstorming 101 exercises. It should begin small, perhaps in management meetings but in the end if employed over time, brainstorming can become a great way to generate the next new sales success story, the next great idea for your store, your district, organization or company. Like Bellaire debate, big ideas start small turning eventually into solid actionable ideas and plans that can serve as weapons of success. I want to spend some time explaining some basic tips to undertake effective brainstorming exercises. They are very easy to employ and as time passes, your teams will become empowered to become part of the planning process that will fulfill team success.

Brainstorming 101: Tips

Be inclusive—this first step is easier said than done. All-inclusive, by definition insists that a majority if not all of your team are actively engaged in the brainstorming process. It demands a commitment to planning the brainstorming session in advance; ensuring that the management team fully understands the goals and the necessary steps in order to make the entire group feel included in the exercise. Giving some instruction in advance in order to assure a high level of productivity can be critical to maintaining the interest of all team members participating or to encourage healthy discussion and an open dialog.

Prepare to be prepared — this seems like a silly step but actually, it is important. Waiting until the day of the brainstorming activity to get ready creates friction between those who have some basic understanding of what you are trying to accomplish and those who did not seem to remember that it was even scheduled that day and those that could probably care less. Depending upon the strengths and weaknesses of your staff or team or of the individuals in your organization, you might have to do a better job of pre-explaining brainstorming to some or pre-selling the concept to the negative apples. Either way, ultimately your success is contingent upon engaging the entire staff in the brainstorming session.

Be prepared to act — talking about what you might do is one thing, but being prepared to try some of it, is another. You have to be willing to try an idea to demonstrate a belief in the process and you have to flex sometimes. Actions that are taken should be based upon a consensus reached within group discussions and the management team should offer their full support as any new ideas or plans of action are committed to. The worst thing you can do is to complete brainstorming sessions, getting people engaged in the conversation and then drop the ball by taking no action whatsoever! You run the risk of wasting the exercise altogether by promising to do something, anything and then sending the message that we will get back to it later.

Be open-minded — everyone likes to believe they are generally open minded but I usually find otherwise. People tend to reject change deferring instead to stay with the status quo. As people provide you with new ideas, your challenge will be to be open to a consideration for change or compromise. Understand that you are accountable for new policies and procedures that might complicate or cloud your real goals or mission.

Think ahead — as with the debate brainstorming process, thinking ahead as to what will happen or what can happen is a big part of the brainstorming 101 exercises. It is not a debate but as you brainstorm, you will be able to get the group eventually to do a better job of thinking their decisions through more completely and considering the unintended consequences of any said or proposed action.

Remember, deliberation is healthy—as you do some intense brainstorming with your staff, it is important that you get feedback from as many people as possible and that you make every effort to deliberate the opportunities—not debate them. Deliberation in and of itself is a very healthy way to reach a true consensus. Not to confuse the opportunity, debate has its time and place, but for the sake of a productive business exercise, deliberation is the most important aspect to achieve success. Deliberation means open discussion versus just achieving a win of a single argument or issue.

A recent example of the intrinsic value of brainstorming occurred before the Christmas break in a facilitating public deliberation class at University of Houston-Downtown. In a subsequent chapter, I will go into detail about another big door that opened recently while working with the Kettering Foundation in Ohio. In the meantime, for the purposes of demonstrating the power of a simple brainstorming activity my professor and I, Dr. Windy Lawrence came back from this forum more determined than ever to apply a brainstorming exercise on the final day of class as a way to seek a call to action. The exercise was in an effort to reach some consensus pertaining to a national issue that we had deliberated that semester concerning higher education. Although we only had about forty-five minutes that day to brainstorm, it was as if she too had debated at Bellaire. She extended the opportunity for me to conduct the session, but I deferred. Instead, she led the session, and the ideas began to flow like water from a waterfall from the students.

As a result, several new ideas are being considered, further brainstorming activity is scheduled and recommendations will now be made in the future to conduct two more deliberations. The process of deliberation works well and it is one you can begin to use immediately within your organization, company or in your personal life and brainstorming is just as effective in that activity as it is in the examples we are looking at.

The most recent example of the importance of brainstorming occurred in my senior speech writing class in my final semester. For two years, I wanted to sign up for a class from Dr. Hank Roubicek. His reputation for excellence is undisputed. I was committed to taking at least one class from him before I graduated. Dr. Roubicek, a writer himself, has taught at the University of Houston-Downtown for thirty plus years now in the Communication department. I was in the process of completing some research for a series I was writing entitled "What makes a Professor or Instructor GREAT, According to UHD Students," for the school newspaper. His editing skills are impeccable, his speech writing skills are legendary and if you look at "Rate My Professor" (which I would do with some great trepidation), you will confirm that his students feel they learn a lot from him, and they respect him.

During completing research for a project, I solicited anonymous votes from two hundred student surveys as to who their favorite professor at UHD was. My purpose was to provide a fair and reasonable way to select a few from the university to feature, as I continued writing the series reflecting what students think is, "Great," in an instructor. His name continued to come up as one of the favorites. I stopped one evening in November, and set the bulk of my research collateral in a pile on the floor, except for comments that listed his name from a student on a survey. His pile was one of the largest. As I read each one, I grasped the reason to take his class, a class I did not need because it was clear that it would be a door worth knocking on.

The most compelling reasons listed included; "He is a teacher who teaches," "He doesn't talk at me, he talks to me," "I find that I never want to miss his class," "He taught me things that have really helped me a lot in my new job." "He does what he says he will do and he is always accessible," and finally, my personal favorite, "I used his brainstorming technique at work and after a two hour session I was told by one of my bosses, "You are going to make it in this business."

Convinced I had read enough, only needing two classes to complete my degree, I chose his class first and filled in three others and an internship to complete a full load. Normally, I talk a lot in class, but as I sat through his first three class lectures, I rarely said a word. What he was saying was much more important than what I was thinking. In the third class meeting, the subject was . . . yes, brainstorming. I was sitting on the front row listening to him, spending twelve to fifteen hours a day trying to finalize my edits, thinking that I had this chapter wrapped up. After all, as the Bellaire brainstorming training was about as intense a brainstorming session repeated over and over again for three years as one could handle.

I listened as he explained the brainstorming process step-by-step and then demonstrated how to do it by completing an exercise that he knows has the potential to affect our careers for many years to come. Sitting in class that morning helped me fine-tune this chapter with a fresh perspective, one no longer centered on a great debate coach, a great debater or a great debate school. Instead, one based upon learning and applying a specific intellectual strategy in order to take advantage of opportunities. His teaching method reminded me that it is best to start with the basics by utilizing a simple brainstorming exercise and then master the process over time, grasping the benefits it has to offer. I realized that I needed to provide some specific examples that allow you to see how the process works at a basic level and at an advanced level. I reminded myself that you would probably not be writing an affirmative debate case in order to compete against another debate team; you will be brainstorming ideas for your own personal and business successes in life. As he completed his brainstorming activity that day, lights came on all around me as the room of students seemed to understand how to select future topics for their speech and I knew I had opened a door when I signed up for his class. His door is one marked with an "S" for success.

I encourage entrepreneurs, business professionals, large companies and small businesses alike to begin using a technique of brainstorming as a method to plan, execute and achieve great results and to make sensible decisions. You will find as you brainstorm with your team many actionable ideas will begin to surface. Arguably, the failure of many businesses is due to poor planning, poor execution or poor management. They are due to an unwillingness or inability to think through a plan, to brainstorm in detail each time you deliberate, and to consider all of the consequences or obstacles that might limit one's success.

I have made note over the years how brainstorming dramatically improved the chance of avoiding pitfalls. In the company that I worked in for twenty-four years, brainstorming 101 served us well, as we were charged with writing and developing training manuals, writing a handbook vital to our proprietary business, and as we rolled out a recognition program for five hundred stores. The same procedure we utilized through brainstorming exercises can serve any organization well. It requires preparation, time, follow through and execution in order to maximize both the short term and long term results. Let us take look at some basics, as we get ready to prepare you to try some brainstorming activities that might help you open a door of opportunity.

Brainstorming 101: The Basics (One Hour)

- Write down one general topic or subject using <u>one word only</u>
- Brainstorm what you can think of to describe that ONE word for 5 minutes
- It is important everyone keeps calling out what comes to their mind, fast, keep going until you have recorded as much as you can in those 3 to 5 minutes and the board should be very full. If someone slows down, then they may be thinking too much, just focus upon throwing out everything that comes to mind, and keep writing it all down quickly

- Select one off shoot (one concept) that deals with that subject content
- Now take 5 minutes and brainstorm every question that comes to mind concerning that topic, go quickly, utilize open-ended questions-go fast!
- Connect the questions that have been brainstormed to the main topic by putting together the three best questions agreed upon by the group
- Discuss it logically with the group. What three questions tie together or belong together to make one subject matter or one statement for discussion?
- Organize the three questions in a logical order as if you might be writing a speech or a thesis
- You are now prepared to conduct the next session or to prepare for the next session where you discuss the details pertaining to the three questions established

Brainstorming Exercise #2 (One Hour)

- Write down one statement or sentence that is brainstormed by the group
- Spend 10-15 minutes writing as many words or topics as you can brainstorm
- There should many ideas flowing with lots of writing on the board, as no idea is unimportant. Make sure you write everything down and if it slows down, speed it back up. Ask them questions to keep it going, faster, faster and faster! Open their minds completely by encouraging an open, fast-paced recording of any idea they can offer
- Pick the three broadest sentences or statements pertaining to the topic to brainstorm in detail
- Take 10 minutes for each of the three sentences or ideas and brainstorm everything you can about each sentence using the same brainstorming procedure noted above

"Major Opportunities"

- Now, pick the one topic that makes the most sense to brainstorm as an action item, get rid of the other two and you are prepared to conduct a second brainstorming session later to discuss a call to action, an action plan, what you are going to do, how you will do it, etc . . .

Brainstorming 102: Bigger-Better-Best

This is a more advanced brainstorming technique; often it allows major or long-term actions implemented as a result to offer tangible, measurable results. It requires better planning and better preparation but it will generally assist a group to reach bigger, broader solutions to problems or to identify major opportunities. It broaches something along the lines of some of the debater sessions in which I participated. Brainstorming 102 sessions require a minimum of two hours in the first session, followed by two, 45 minute to one hour sessions. Generally, the smaller the group, the more productive it can be.

This advanced, targeted brainstorming exercise can be extremely effective in management meetings, group goal planning, best practices discussions, or in any kind of planning activity. It should be completed with those either who have had previous exposure to a brainstorming exercise or when the process has been previously explained in detail and by conducting a practice brainstorming activity when you built up to a point where you actually complete a full brainstorming exercise. I promise you as you work through the steps from meeting to meeting from project to project you will find that your team will always come away feeling involved, engaged, and challenged with all three providing positive outcomes.

It is critical to this process that the mental stage is set by the moderator for EVERYONE to actively participate in a method of rapid fire, shotgun approach, being encouraged to fire out any and all ideas relevant, one after another, pertaining to the topic (s) being discussed in an open forum setting. From the very beginning of this first session, it is imperative that participants are encouraged, even pressured to come up with lots and lots of ideas that are all recorded on a large chalkboard or on large pieces of 22 by 28 paper as fast as they are thrown out. Using a second person to record ideas is a good method to keep the pace high. Every time the ideas begin to slow, the moderator must keep the flow of ideas coming out. The main objective is to get and keep their minds working, to keep their intellectual juices flowing throughout the entire process. This process should continue for 45 minutes to an hour. Then the moderator should lead the group as they brainstorm each idea presented, focusing upon its appeals and concerns and then on its legitimacy to work. At the end of this second hour, the primary goal is to have identified the two most viable options or solutions to discuss in the next brainstorming session.

A third forty-five minute to one hour brainstorming session should be conducted within a week or so, to discuss in greater detail those top two or three ideas agreed upon by the group as the best. That session should go more smoothly because by now they understand the process. The jokes tend to reduce significantly but the moderator's role is still very critical to the effectiveness of the session. The whole point is to get everyone engaged, participating, contributing and work as a group to produce a sound idea. This strategy will work across the spectrum of most businesses and organizations. In the end, participants feel actively involved in the process and ultimately accept accountability for best practices that are applied. Your main priority to accomplish in this third brainstorming session is a "Call to Action."

No matter what this form of discussion, collaboration and dialog is constructive pertaining to thoughtful and creative design. It is a process that can easily be undertaken and applied in all groups, organizations and businesses as an effective strategy to reach consensus, to involve a team in a healthy process and ultimately as a way to exercise the wonderful brains we are all blessed with to open doors wide open.

~ Chapter 9 ~

"The 7 Building Blocks of Major Opportunity"

One of the keys to producing a consistent record of success pertains to building things in a way that they can become permanent, "Building to stay Built," is how I refer to it. This requires the right building blocks assembled in order to create structures made to last with or without the original builder still being in place. You build one block on top of another, relying upon a solid foundation. Even a child can comprehend a simple formula like this with one big difference. Have you ever watched a child play with building blocks? I certainly have with five kids of my own. Typically, he or she just keeps on placing blocks one on top of another stacking them as high as they can go, they just keep on building. Of course, eventually they will just knock them all down and start over at some point either in frustration or perhaps just to make you laugh again. That is what a good builder of business does, they keep building and they keep stacking upon a foundation of building blocks except they do not tear it down like a child, on purpose. Instead, they move on to build something else, usually bigger and better leaving proof of a great builder behind them.

An effective manager or leader is one that does not have to be overbearing or beat it out of their employees in an effort to succeed. Rather, they build a team, with a lasting success in mind usually through finding great people as the foundation and by showing them the doors of opportunity through effective training, development and motivational techniques. They build strong buildings by laying down a solid foundation of opportunity blocks that lay a base for the future. One way to accomplish that task is through the effective use of "company depth charts." as a reliable method to prepare and plan for the future personnel needs of any organization or company. The leaders of any company are the ones that are accountable and responsible for building a bench of good employees that allows them to offer a Plan A and a Plan B. Accordingly, my counterpart and I, Pat Bowman, applied the same philosophy and level of accountability to each of our twenty-eight district managers.

Although constant high turnover is an everyday reality in the retail world, we began each quarter to utilize exception reports as a way drill down into a district, store or region, as the best way to identify where "Major Opportunities," existed. Before we get into seven specific building blocks of success, it is important we address turnover specifically. Turnover is the one disease that plagues every single company. If you stop and look at it empirically, turnover in any group of people is a self-fulfilling prophecy of failure that will cause defeat after defeat. You just keep starting over repeatedly, going through the same motions of finding another new employee, hoping that the next one

"Major Opportunities"

hired sticks with you. Other companies have mastered how to effectively reduce turnover, Pat and I mastered it, and so can your management team. You simply have to have a master plan as consistent turnover wastes an incredible amount of time and resources within any company or organization. Quite honestly, you have to establish the reason(s) turnover is happening and then take the appropriate steps to minimize it going forward.

One way of offering sound advice for you in this chapter is by examining the way we tackled the "Major Opportunities," at Stage Stores Inc. over the years. As you might imagine, in a large retail company, turnover is a battle. In 2002, after successfully emerging from bankruptcy, Ernie, Pat and me decided to apply a pro-active approach to reducing turnover among store staffing by examining in great detail the turn-over results each month by store, by district, by region and by territory. We compared the data to company averages, district averages and by regional averages. We relied upon some very precise exception reports produced by Tom Buttaccio, a brilliant man who played a major role in keeping store operations on track during the merger of two great companies into one, in the 80's. As pressure mounted upon Pat and I to maximize payroll, we felt we needed to get to the root cause of turnover. Once we did, we were able to reduce the number dramatically over the next four or five years. We accomplished that feat by digging our heels in, by listening and by becoming more objective with ourselves.

In many cases, it was simply a matter of holding our management teams accountable. In some cases, it took a firmer hand in order to get that message out; we called that a counseling session. As we explore "Major Opportunities," in this chapter concerning how to build a solid foundation in a company, it is important to understand that keeping great people in your organization is one of the greatest determining factors in achieving your goals. We will examine in these next few pages, seven building blocks that if stacked correctly, can lay a foundation permitting any company to sustain most any challenge. All of the blocks depend almost entirely upon hiring, training, maintaining and rewarding great people.

The first few building blocks we will talk about include interviewing, hiring and training. We will also examine the importance of promotions and specifically, developing from within so that you can promote from within your organization. We will explore the importance of annual reviews, providing regular feedback. We will also address one of the most difficult topics—counseling to improve performance and finally, completing terminations and separations, with dignity. Throughout our exploration, we will examine how to apply proven best practices as a way to maximize results, to promote teamwork and as a way to minimize interruptions to achieving the goals your organization has set.

Building Block 1
"Interviewing for Keeps"

The building blocks of success will last when they rely upon a foundation comprised of quality employees hired through effective interviewing techniques. Understanding and mastering interviewing 101 basics is an essential ingredient in any effort to locate the best candidate and therefore, it presents some "Major Opportunities," to interview for employees that you can hold on to, for keeps! Over many years spent in the retail world, I have had occasion to interview literally thousands of potential applicants and I must admit that everyone was unique and every interview was different in some distinct way. The best interviews were the ones that began on time, those that stayed on track and those that allowed me to develop a reasonable opinion as to how a candidate might fit the position he or she was interviewing for or what he or she might bring to the table.

I have overheard someone after an interview make the mistake by declaring to the world, "That's going to be a great hire

"Major Opportunities"

or a great employee, I am just sure of it." Truthfully, it is almost impossible to tell at that early point whether or not that is true, there are so many factors left to determine their success. One thing is for sure, companies that focus upon effective interviewing are usually the ones that have the lowest company turnover.

When we speak of hiring the right people as one of the key building blocks, it is important to address some basics. Common mistakes that may occur when it comes to effective interviewing are: not having enough time to spend with an applicant, not pre-screening an application well, relying upon someone that has not been trained well, being left by themselves to determine what "great" is in an employee is and not taking time to obtain a reference check. Many an interview has turned out to be unproductive because the one doing the interview did not give the applicant even one thought provoking question or did not stop talking long enough to listen to what they had to say; sometimes you just have to shut up and listen.

There are many good books that provide cheat sheet interview questions. Knowing what to ask and learning how to ask it concisely is an important step in conducting any productive first interview. I learned many years ago from Bob Hart, back in Tyler, that a good test for what kind of feeling you get from the interview is to ask yourself, "Would I work for this person?" "Do they remind you of anyone, like yourself?" "Would you be proud to introduce them to your boss on their next visit to the store?" Interviews can be too short and they can be too long. They are too short if you do not gain the opportunity to assess their match to a position or to your need. They are too long if they know a lot about you and yet you still do not know much about them. The best hiring decisions I made usually always came after two interviews. The worst decisions I made came when I was in a bind, when I had to have spaces with warm bodies. This mindset of, "hire a warm body," is a formula for high turnover, for theft and will end up wasting valuable time and resources for everyone involved. The first interview is meant to be a pre-screen of a candidate, the second is to narrow down the choice to the very best candidate. Here is a list of possible questions that one might use in order to insure a productive interview session.

"Major Opportunities," Interview Questions

1. Why are you here today? What prompted your interest in this job?
2. Give me the one word that best describes you and tell me why?
3. Tell me about a time when you have failed? What happened?
4. What is the one accomplishment you are most proud of so far in your life?
5. What characteristics in your co-workers bother you the most?
6. How do you take advantage of your strengths? How do you offset weaknesses?
7. What would your current boss say is your greatest strength?
8. Tell me about one of your mentors, what stands out about him or her?
9. What is the one thing that you would like to improve about yourself?
10. What changes have you made when it applies to working with others?
11. What do you think are the most important traits of successful people?
12. On what basis do you make decisions? What factors affect your decisions?
13. If you were limited to one person to get advice from, whom would you choose?
14. Where will you be ten years from now?
15. Describe a crisis you have faced at work. What happened? How did you resolve it?

16. Describe a time when you were asked to do something you were not trained to do.
17. Describe the best boss you have had. Why?
18. What will make you love coming to work here every day?
19. What would you do if management made a decision you did not agree with?
20. What is there about this opportunity that most excites you?
21. What is your greatest fear about this opportunity?
22. Please give me three reasons I should hire you today!
23. What questions do you have for me?

In an effort to employ effective interviewing techniques, it is important you prepare well in advance, that you keep the first interview to between thirty and forty five minutes, that you do not take notes on an application, that you avoid asking questions prohibited or protected by law, and that you do not make a commitment you cannot fulfill. The most important thing you can accomplish in a first interview is to develop a strong sense about their people skills, their potential to help your organization, to evaluate their attitude and to determine whether he or she might be both a good fit and match for the job and for your organization.

Advice for the Interviewee

I have offered feedback and advice concerning effective interviewing but I also felt it was important to offer feedback to the other side of the table as well. What would I do if I were the one in the hot seat as, the interviewee? I took some time to ponder that question. I decide to provide some advice to those of you sitting in that hot seat.

How you dress, how you look, matters to most of the people that are making hiring decisions. First impressions still play a major role in whether or not there is a second interview granted. Do you remember the first job I asked for back in 1983 in Houston at Bealls Department Store? I put on my best suit, well; it was one of my only suits therefore, I put my best foot forward as I made the effort to act as if I wanted a job. Although there are different opinions pertaining to the perfect resume, you do need one and it needs to be neat and organized. It needs to have on it what will stand out as what is worth talking about. Limiting a resume to one page is not a bad idea. Honestly, the younger you are, the more I would emphasize that it is important to accomplish things that are right things to do as it serves the purpose of strengthening one's resume well. Volunteer work, special certifications, special classes, leadership activities all contribute to nice talking points on a resume. The use of buzz words are important to make sure your resume stands out to the reader.

Third, looking the person interviewing you in the eyes when you answer questions or when you speak is important in any interview you do. Remember, they are not trying to persuade you to hire them it is quite the opposite as you are the one that needs a job. Persuasion is in the eyes of the beholder, so communicate with them directly and it will leave them with the right lasting impression. Fourth, make sure you leave with them knowing that you do want the job and that you will dedicate yourself to it. Ultimately, you have to stand out as an applicant that the one interviewing you believes can help their organization succeed, so tell me why you will.

Exit interviews-A tool to reduce Turnover!

The initial interviewing process, the questions you ask, the answers you obtain are all critical to making good hiring decisions but often just as important is to maintain great employees by completing exit interviews. Exit interviews with employees that have given their notice as intent to leave employment with your organization, whether they are short term or long-term employees is an important tool. Exit interviews are a means of reaching an understanding, even an acceptance as to why people leave an organization. Constant turnover means constantly having to find a new person; it is a vicious cycle especially where turnover is higher than the industry average within any part of an organization.

I do not think there are many companies that apply consistency when it comes to utilizing exit interviews. I made them an important part of my own introspection. It often appears that we are ashamed sometimes to ask why an employee is leaving. We may be caught saying, "Let's just move on and get another one now, they did not work out or it was time for them to leave anyway." What a waste of time and resources that mind-set places into motion. We do not take the time, we do not care or we blame it on a bad hiring decision or a bad attitude on their part, maybe upon the inability of the one leaving to fit in or any number of silly excuses to shuffle the blame to someone else's shoulders besides our own, where it belongs. Nine times out of ten, it belongs on the back of the management team when it comes right down to it. When you lose someone that you took precious time to interview, hire and train, then they leave meaning you failed too so find out why they are leaving.

Insisting upon exit interviews became paramount to progress at Stage Stores Inc. during re-emergence from bankruptcy. It became our major opportunity to determine why people were leaving, a way to help change the "culture," by fighting the notion we could ever accept turnover as just a painful part of retail. Companies are guilty of glossing over turnover instead of finding out why it keeps happening or why is it worse in an area of responsibility. Exit interviews are invaluable as a useful form of constructive self-evaluation that may go unused or under-utilized. Exit interviews can provide a useful tool to help step off a treadmill of hire, train, replace, hire, train, and replace.

To hire someone is to make a statement you believe in them and that you believe in his or her potential to become one of your stars. You have a significant role in the process when you make the decision to hire them and then they do not turn out the way you wanted or they leave suddenly; you were indeed an active participant in failure. Take it all personally, because it is personal and it is a reflection of failure in some way on your part.

Most people that accept accountability for their hiring decisions complete exit interviews. They are able to look in their mirror of hiring and training practices and are able to determine why the breakdown occurred when an employee exits. Hold yourself accountable when people leave but you have to find out why they left.

Sometimes, we have to take a look at ourselves!

I never thought I would add this section in but I must. I will be talking in the next few pages about hiring, training and keeping the best employees. I will be discussing promotions, reviews and counseling as a way to improve performance. However, I am compelled to talk briefly about an obligation we have as management, to look inside our door of opportunity in order to objectively see how others, see us. Years ago, Bealls conducted an annual "Opinion Survey." Mailed directly to the stores, employees completed an anonymous survey that was sealed and sent to the corporate office for review. The results, confidentially tabulated, recorded and sent back in a report offered a way understand how a majority of our staffs felt about us. I must admit that it was a painful process due to the uncertainty and the opportunity it afforded those that were unhappy, to take a stab at any one of us in the back.

In retrospect, it was an important process. Eventually we discontinued it perhaps due to pressure from us whining managers or maybe it was due to a budget cut. Nevertheless, I think an avenue of feedback like this is important, even today. It does matter what a majority of your employees think about you, especially when one understands that usually, they really want to make you happy and they want to remain loyal.

In 2006, for one reason or another (I believe it was Ernie's idea) Pat and I agreed to ask the district managers to review us. Looking inside ourselves for "Major Opportunities," they completed a similar feedback survey on us as Store Directors. It was actually an incredible process; it seems fair that since I get to evaluate them, they should also have an opportunity to provide some feedback. In retrospect, it was a healthy exercise as it offered valuable insight into what others saw as my strengths and weaknesses. It allowed us to compare the feedback with what our self-evaluation reflected and of course, Ernie analyzed it. In the end, the results were not a surprise for the most part and I suggest that any company should consider taking a long objective look at themselves through the eyes of their people. They must be willing to open a door of success demonstrated by willingness to request, study, accept and apply what they thought in order to continue to grow as a team.

Building Block 2
"Hiring the Best"

Making a transition from conducting an effective interview with a potential candidate to making the final decision to hire him or her is often difficult and taken for granted. The decision made in the hiring process is one of your biggest doors of opportunity to guarantee that your organization has the best employees you can find. Too often, there is a rush to give a hire a simple okay, a nod indicating I have someone to fill the slot now. In my opinion, that is a critical mistake. The best practice to reduce these mistakes include; having two people assess the candidate, visiting with the other person about their assessment without telling them what you think and taking the time to decide if there is a good job fit. There is a difference between job match and job fit. One candidate may possess the skills you deem as important for one in order to be a good match for the job you have available. On the other hand, he or she may or may not be a good fit to your company.

In the case of retail clothing, an applicant may dress well for the interview, he or she may be well groomed, or he or she may be able to answer all the questions in the interview adequately, reflecting a possible job match. On the other hand, they may be timid in some of their responses, he or she may appear to be introverted or may indicate that they do not like to pressure people or they hated pressure applied in a previous job. The candidate might be a good job match as they may have the right look and the right answers but the fact the potential job requires applying pressure on the sales floor yet they have issues with pressuring people in general may be an indication this candidate is not a good job fit for the position you are filling. All too often, I find jobs filled too quickly without a proper thought process applied to producing the right match and the right fit. In the end, this results in a countless wasting of man-power hours and training time, only to lose the employee down the road, only to start the rigorous ordeal all over again.

Now having told you some of the pitfalls, as much as I hate negative, please allow me to share some positive ways to make a good hiring decision. This advice is based upon years of learning from mistakes, from some bad hiring decisions of my own and from observations and outcomes. All of these experiences helped me to reach a point where I am right much more than I am wrong now about the person pertaining to his or her potential to meet the needs I am looking for. Please be aware that there are hidden jewels called employees, secretly waiting for the one opportunity to excel, to become your major opportunity to succeed but either they have to open the door or you do. The fact that they are asking counts, after all, they are at knocking at the door. As I have repeatedly emphasized so far, asking is very important. Most assuredly, in many cases, you were not the first person they asked for a job. Take your time; you are looking for the best.

Over the years as I built elite "Top Gun" teams of employees I can recall saying to potential applicants repeatedly in an interview that we just may not be for everyone — that we are looking for the very best and often I might look him or her in the eyes and say, "Are you that person, are you the best?" Sometimes the answer was, "I think so," sometimes it was, "I would like to think so," occasionally it was, "I believe I can be," most often it was, "I sure hope so," but the answer I was looking for was always, "I am that

"Major Opportunities"

person." Many times my response would be, "Then step right inside this door of major opportunity, I have a job for you."

Building Block 3
"Training them to Stay"

Once again, there are resources available that tell you how to do, what to do, and how to train the perfect little foot soldier. In the end, the single most effective training technique is for management to show an interest starting from the top down in their success from the moment they arrive for that first day at work. If you are committed to hiring the best, surely you are just as committed to training a new employee to be the best. Sometimes, I fear the art of training has become somewhat archaic and certainly antiquated with companies beginning to rely more and more upon a magic wand that they wave at a new employee and poosh, they are done, all trained now. This of course, could not be farther from the truth and can easily be changed by the one who interviewed them, by the one who hired them or by the person training them. They all have to stay involved in the process not just hand the employee off to someone else and move on to the next hiring decision. Hiring and then training the best requires that the training manager is aware that he or she is coming for training that day, it requires a professional introduction to a department and to some of the responsibilities, it requires checking in several times each of their first few days and weeks in their new job. This purposeful strategy for success as a way to obtain a measurement of the level of comfort they might have is also an effective way to determine how they are connected with the job itself.

It also requires consistent feedback. The first ninety days of employment are critical to keeping an employee inside the door of success by providing praise, feedback and ongoing bits of additional training. The new employee has to know what he or she needs to improve upon so that they begin to fill the role you hired them to fill. As a way of working during the year to complete an annual review, many companies underestimate the importance of early feedback to a new hire or even a newly promoted management associate. For whatever reason, new employees slip through the crack too often and become a great employee for someone else.

Thirty, sixty and ninety day feedback is critical to long term success for a new employee within any organization and it also provides a starting place for their annual review months later. Assigning them a co-worker to spend some time within the first thirty days is a productive way of increasing their chance of survival. Companies are too willing to just throw the employee out on the floor and hope they sink or swim. That is a formula for disaster and it will result in high turnover, theft, low morale and frustration for other top performing employees that still need help with completing operational tasks.

Too often in my retail experience I have watched employees come and go without even knowing why they were let go, not knowing what they did that was so wrong. We owe it to them to stay inside the process with them otherwise we are spinning our wheels. Once hired, once trained, it is time to begin giving them specialized training. That requires one thing from you as their manager, time. Time is your most valuable commodity to share with your employee. It grants you the ability to tell them what to do or how to do it, it allows you the chance to teach them how you do it, how you did it. The best way to train is through the example you set and it is one of the best ways you can gain the respect necessary to your growth and development as well.

Second, after you have decided to hire an employee the training process becomes their practice for how they will do. With payroll cuts, tighter payroll control, reduction of training time for new employees it has become increasingly challenging to train a new employee. No matter how much time is allotted to train, the training must be tied into insuring his or her survival during the first thirty to sixty days of employment. One way to accomplish that is by training the trainer. It is too easy especially in a busy establishment to simply assign a trainer and then just walk away, never realizing that without supervision they may begin to teach their way as the right way. Therefore, you do not even understand why employees are not following company procedure or why they become pre-occupied with completing operational items that can interfere with the focus on results. Making sure training manuals are current, updated and that a fresh person takes over training in order to avoid burn out is important to the training process in any organization.

Building Block 4
"Counseling to Improve Performance"

One of the most difficult building blocks to utilize as a foundation for development among staffing involves the use of effective and meaningful counseling as a way to affect performance standards. Most of us do not enjoy reprimanding others much less communicating the negative feedback that it requires. Setting aside the fact that documentation of employee counseling is critical to fairly enforcing the rules it is also important to keep employees safely within the boundaries of a standard of conduct, promoting an acceptable productivity within any organization. Although companies may employ a variety of different forms to provide documentation or employ their own pre-determined policies and procedures, it is important that all management is trained to conduct employee counseling in a way in which the behavior can be modified without causing an employee to turn against the system itself or against the organization itself. Counseling should be utilized as a building block of success and it should not become an obstacle to success. Counseling is an opportunity to improve performance because it can help limit poor practices, while conditioning with praise as the primary re-enforcement for your best practices.

All kinds of counseling for all kinds of circumstances

There are several kinds of counseling. First, there is a verbal counseling. Although documented, it relies upon an informal discussion with an employee as the attempt is made to identify and to call out a need for change without sitting down formally and pressing the issue. Although, it is true that generally counseling is most effective when held in private in order to avoid the risk of embarrassment, doing a verbal warning is much less dramatic. It allows you to appear more as a coach and then you pat them on the back and send them back in the game. This more predictable coaching experience is even more effective when you actually move on and avoid the whole, "I am uncomfortable around you feeling."

No matter what, the counseling must be presented and perceived as something that the coach sees as potentially only improving the employees overall contribution to the operation. It is documented as a verbal conversation with a date attached to it but no signature is required by the employee making it informal, lending the outcome as a by-product of an effective practice session. Rest assured, if another employee is breaking the same rule and you ignore it, you are a hypocrite and you place your organization at risk on many levels.

A written counseling is a one on one sit down counseling session conducted in private with a witness, preferably from the opposite sex of the one completing the counseling. Entirely too often, these types of counseling sessions end up being conducted when the coach or manager is angry at a response or at an action by the employee. Instead, any counseling with this intensity should be conducted later when cooler heads prevail, when proper notes and documentation have been prepared and when the counseling session has been well thought out. It needs to be presented as constructive criticism to improve performance, not as a threat to an employee. However, since this is not the first incident nor is it the first time the issue has been addressed, it is more serious and is therefore it is always documented. It should come across to the employee that it is important to you that this issue is resolved. It is important you are able to obtain some form of acknowledgement from the employee that they recognize the existence of a problem and that they are willing to make a commitment to change. Everyone involved in the process should sign off a written counseling. Securing documentation in a locked file cabinet is mandatory.

Providing the employee with a copy of the counseling and following up with the employee later after observing change or observing their reaction is important to re enforce positive change, thereby achieving the goal of modifying their behavior to insure they become productive once again. Sometimes they will refuse to sign it and that is ok, what matters most is that you come to an agreement or acceptance that the employee accepts there is an issue and makes a commitment to make a genuine effort to correct the issue or it will be addressed further.

Avoid sending mixed messages by sugar coating a written counseling by telling them all the things they do right first, that's not why they are in there in the first place, that's actually why they still have a job. That should be done often separate and apart from correcting poor performance, but it is not a way to soften the blow of a written counseling session and that should have been done already, that's how you should have gained their respect and built your own credibility. Professionalism, articulation through your voice and facial expression can help the counseling session move in the right direction.

Occasionally the next step in performance modification or counseling is necessary and as a result, a final written warning may have to be completed. The employee must have an appropriate amount of time to demonstrate change. What is not acceptable is a prevailing attitude that reflects resistance through idle gossip, sulking or any verbal or non-verbal open blatant disregard for management including any kind of a showing of a major bad attitude, a form of insubordination. Teaming up with HR is always important, previous documentation is very relevant and finally, making sure you treat everyone with the same standard is important. It is very important that the employee knows exactly what they are doing is wrong with specific examples provided, that they agree with an issue that needs some improvement, and that they make a commitment to make an effort to improve within a REASONABLE time frame. Without these key items, the written counseling has not been effective and will not usually effectively alter a pattern of employee behavior.

Obstacles that may impede effective counseling sessions include; a lack of proper specific information pertaining to an offense; completing the counseling session when you are not prepared, completing a counseling when you are angry, not utilizing a witness, not obtaining a proper level of acceptability that there is an issue, and enforcing the rules with one but not with another. Insubordination is the least acceptable form of behavior. It can easily render the morale of a team to its lowest point if not kept at bay consistently. When you make an exception for one over another you should feel a sense of guilt as if a lawsuit is pending because you opened that door yourself and it is a door marked with a big T, called trouble.

To be completely honest about it, completing counseling sessions is not a fun process. It is never fun to tell someone when they are not doing well, that feedback is usually reserved for our children. It is much easier to hope they stop misbehaving or to try to explain it for them or perhaps some of us just go about our own business and ignore it altogether. In that scenario, you are sending them a message that it is okay to misbehave until you are fed-up, then you blast them and the real message you send is the wrong one in that they were yelled at because you too are having a bad day. These words of wisdom I am sharing with you, like most words of wisdom with age, occur due to making mistakes, the same ones I am trying to help you avoid or overcome. Just make different mistakes each time, keep applying what you learn from those mistakes and you will be just fine.

Building Block 5 "Motivation 101: Doing it through others"

I want you to understand that when it comes to retaining great employees, to maintaining high morale, when it comes to the effective motivation of others, a focus upon making it a FUN place to work should be a top priority. Fun is an important factor in any organization, big or small. If fun does not motivate one of your employees, you just might have the wrong employee working for you. Not always defined by money, but defined by uniqueness and creativity applied to every challenge you make by building a place your employees desire to return to every day. Fun is as simple as you make it. The same idea of fun does not often work a second or third time. Just because something motivates once does not in any way mean it will work again. The brainstorming chapter offers assistance as you deliberate how to apply creativity in your attempts to motivate.

Next, I refused to lose because I hate losing. I heard it said in sports experiences over the years, "It's not winning that matters, it's how you play the game." Nonsense! Rubbish, I say! Winning matters, it always matters, otherwise why even play the game, I always asked myself? Now winning dishonestly or winning without being a good sport about it or even winning and rubbing it in are indeed issues that speak to one's character and of course, good coaches insist on winning with humility. People, who suggest that life is not all about winning, do not usually win enough to brag about it. Winning is the goal, it is fun, it is rewarding and it is what matters. Vince Lombardi, a great pro football coach had very strong opinions of his own about winning. He said two things that I remember well. First, he said, "Winning isn't everything, it's the only thing." Second, he said, "If winning isn't everything, why do they keep score?" Sports and competitive activities often rely upon winning to define ultimate success. Why do they keep score? They keep score because the final score of a game measure success.

As a strategy, I developed employees that I called, "Top Guns," that by them-selves could guarantee a win on any given day they were present. I will discuss them in great detail for you soon. Although a manager or district manager may too often rely on a small number of high achievers to make them look good, in the end the very best strategy to follow is one that accepts that it take the entire team but it starts with finding leaders who lead by example. It takes both approaches to dominate. When you inspire the entire team, you usually win. This business strategy has worked in every position, at every level in my career span and it will work for you as well. One of the best examples that I can think of was when I moved from Jasper, Texas to manage the Corpus store. The Jasper Bealls was doing $2.4 million versus the Corpus store volume producing $8 million per year when I arrived. In Corpus, the solicitation of charge accounts was well below company average and the store was not merchandised well at all, it was a mess. There was an obvious opportunity as I did have about eighty employees on the sales floor and more management than I knew what to do with.

I assessed my team's sales strengths in Corpus and determined that I had about ten high potential people that I could develop into super stars. "Top Guns," as I referred to these star potential individuals consisted of those that typically demonstrated the potential, the drive and some base desire to lead by example. I scheduled a meeting with all ten of them. Sitting in my office, I explained a vision for success with each of them. I reminded the entire group with reasonable arguments supported by statistics justified the importance opening of new Bealls cards was to the future of the store, to the company, to them and to me. I told them I needed them and that. I showed them how much extra money they could earn by opening more new accounts each day by providing mathematical examples of the formula. I reminded them it was a major part of their job. I told them that I had identified them as employees that I thought could be on the top

"Major Opportunities"

twenty reports each month in new accounts for the chain. I told them how high of an honor it is to be on that report and that we would celebrate their success together.

Seeking to create an elite force on the floor, I purposely encouraged them not to go back on the floor and tell others that they were now my favorites, but that they did need to understand I was building an elite group of "Top Guns," beginning with them, that I personally picked them. I saw smiles on some faces that reflected they clearly understood the pride and honor they should feel. I asked them to take a few minutes and contemplate their individual commitment in terms of how much they wanted to make extra this month. I suggested they refer to the sheets I had posted on the wall that reflected how much they could add in dollars based upon how many they accounts opened in a given month. I also threw in a carrot as they could pick a prize of their choice, value of $50 if they hit their individual goal for the month and I would personally. give it to them One more caveat I threw in, I wrote one total number that I wanted, which was the equivalent to obtaining 40% of our store goal on the wall on a 22 by 28 piece of paper. I told them that their individual numbers had to add up to one more than my total. We needed TEAM success in this "Top Gun" force.

I then left the room telling them I would be back, to take their time as they made their commitment. I told all of them that I needed a number written next to my number upon my return. I came back in thirty minutes and I had each one of them supply their number as they indicating the prize they were working for. The number they wrote next to mine was 10 higher. I told them I was ready for them to achieve what they had committed to, first for themselves, second our store and third for me. Some of the prizes on their wish list were memorable including, a golf club, a dog, lessons to learn how to drive, new car mats for a grandmother's old truck. I made it clear the money for their prizes would come out of my pocket. I sensed they understood I too had much to gain from their success as "Top Guns." and I did.

That first month, six of the ten "Top Guns," made the company top twenty reports. We usually had only had one or two in a typical month, meaning I now had to deliver on six of those prizes, which was a lot of fun to do. They also exceeded my number by 36. We gathered for a second meeting the next month to celebrate successes and I suggested that since they had proven they could do it once that I would be glad to accept those results as my new expectation since they had proven they were capable of as much. I added that I would accept their new number plus 10 as the new measure of "Top Gun" group success. Most laughed, a few just smiled, and a few sarcastically muttered, "Thanks a lot, Mr. Slaughter." I said, "You are welcome, my pleasure!" Interestingly, that month they all performed better than the prior month, they ALL raised their goal and they ALL made more money. The bait set in place, that second month, eight of them made the top twenty. We celebrated once again. The third month all ten guns came out blazing and made the top twenty and our store had #1, #2, #3, #4, #5, #8, #9, #12, #13 and #14 on the top 20 report. By now, the "Top Guns" were making more money. As a result, they were paying themselves more by simply doing their job instead of waiting on a raise once a year of five or ten cents per hour.

 I did what I said I would do and as their leader, their coach and their mentor, I was there to remind each of them daily, weekly and monthly that they had proven they were "Top Guns" and therefore I would be glad to continue to pressure them and to praise them all at the same time. Significantly, the store new account production was now exploding, our sales were consistently exceeding the district and the company average and there was a buzz in the air all around the store. Doors were wide open. Going forward, I began to have other employees in the store come to me to ask how they could become a "Top Gun?" I would usually say, "Where is your gun? "Top Guns" always carry a gun, right?" Those who carry this proverbial gun rely upon asking.

 As a leader and as a manager you have to determine what motivates each person because it varies greatly between two people. The prizes have all but been forgotten but I will not forget

"Major Opportunities"

the employees because they made me highly successful by serving as "Top Guns." Getting them to get to the top of the mountain, feeling like winners helped insure they remained winners for a long time to come. Motivation of the individual begins and ends with the individual and when you build a group that sees the big picture, you can dominate the field as we did in Corpus. There are individuals, like myself and one or two of those "Top Gun" folks in Corpus who thrive on winning every single minute of the day, playing as hard as they can, reaping the rewards just to be number one. Most people will achieve success in proportion to the challenge made and based upon how they are recognized and praised.

One of my mature associates in my dress department was Mary Ann. Once when we kicked off an annual new account contest and I had completed a ra-ra session in which we had performed a funny skit for the employees but after we went to the floor, I could sense Mary just was not buying it. Sensing the brainwash was incomplete, I decided to go to her department and visit with her one on. She said that credit was a bad thing in general, that we were placing too much pressure on the employees and the customers to open accounts. I listened patiently and then instead of exploding like I wanted to do because she was rubbing me the wrong way, I decided to invite her to the to the "Top Guns," meeting. I included her as someone that could join my elite team, even though ironically, she was already on my elite team. Perhaps I had neglected to see her guns, I thought to myself. I then introduced her to the group as the newest "Top Gun." As it turns out the prize that she wanted was a trophy for Mary Ann had never won a trophy in her lifetime and I learned that her daughter had several on a mantle at home that Mary Ann saw every single day of the year. Long story short, we had a monthly contest and in a store of top guns having been trained as an elite force for several months prior, Mary came in third in the contest and her prize was . . . yes, a trophy. I have never forgotten this story in Corpus as I will never forget Mary Ann. I bet she still has that trophy on the mantel next to her daughter's trophy too. You have to find what button to push and it is not always money. It usually includes a combination of praise, recognition and reward. I would be glad to tell you how to do it, but I think I just did.

As I will discuss in another chapter, a key to producing a consistent career record of positive results, one that you can look back to in pride, one linked to an ability to build things that last, most often by finding, developing and motivating others like my friends in Corpus Christi. Ernie Cruse, my boss for those seven years believed that one of the better definitions to describe a "successful," manager is one that holds up over time. He referred to it as a better way to achieve long-term results versus, "just beating it out of them."

Promoting from within when you can

On the other side of the coin, promoting someone is always fun. For obvious reasons, every company applies a unique philosophy on how to promote and when to promote into a higher position of responsibility within the organization. No matter what, internal promotions are the most effective tool to motivate, reward, and to grow in a competitive world. Easier said than done, it requires a consistent, fair and balanced strategy of developing depth within the organization at all levels, providing a bench to promote from, allowing promotions to reward others within the existing organization.

Too many companies think they have to go outside their own company to find great talent. They run out, opening doors all around them that scream step right in, we want you to come inside our door of opportunity. When they employ this common practice of outside recruiting, they demoralize their existing troops as they infuse others into the company or organization that have an outside, non-traditional take on things and they may actually water down the potential strength within the organization. They run the risk of closing doors; even slamming open doors shut on dedicated, loyal, hardworking employees that deserve at least a second look. Also as a result, it can hamper, limit, and even destroy a foundation of business, even a "brand," built over many years.

Having said that, it would be naïve for me to say that you must disregard great talent and potential that exists outside of your organization. This door of opportunity must be opened carefully and cautiously. A best practice of recruiting must be utilized as a strategy to transition new talent brought in from outside the organization into the company you have, as a way to assemble a great team. I mean to say your best leaders, not just thrown out to do it on their own, should train them. If not, the real danger exists that more and more new talent will eventually shape, change and alter a solid company or "brand," into something different than it was, and unfortunately, in my experience, that it usually not the way to open a door of success.

Develop employees so you can promote from within!

Having given you all of the advice on the negatives in terms of growth and the pitfalls involved let me spell out an effective strategy for promotions. First, set about a plan of action with your subordinates that helps them be prepared to be the most qualified candidates for promotion. Let me give you the very best advice I can offer you from seeing all of the ups and downs in a huge company when I say to you, promote from within! Open a door for your loyal employees. When you have great people right in front of you, by utilizing the talent you hired, trained and developed. If you do not have them then you have to change that. Normally, they already respect you, they know what to expect from you, and rewarding them is very motivating to your other team members as it presents "Major Opportunities," for everyone down the road.

Second, find a way to mentor your replacement well in advance. If you focus on that as a personal goal then you will improve your chance of promotion, as you will develop a reputation as one capable of finding and developing others for advancement. Third, consider all factors that pertain to promote someone including; seniority, long-term potential, enthusiasm, people skills, intelligence and mobility. Just by having on-going conversations with the people you are developing is inspiring, even if it takes a while for them to receive a promotion.

Building Block 6 "Writing-Conducting Effective Annual Reviews"

No one can underestimate the importance of feedback, specifically annual reviews. Over the years, I had my share of performance reviews and they relied upon a truthful assessment of my strengths with suggestions on how I could continue to grow. I never felt picked on, I always left inspired to do better. Preparation is critical and it pertains to preparation by both parties. The preparation cannot start the night before; and it is critical that each employee is asked to complete a self-evaluation. Although the evaluation completed by you is the one that will count, often it aids in the communication process during the review because often there is general agreement between yours and theirs. Your review with your direct reports is precious time as it is time to deliver what they deserve, a way to grow as an employee. One caveat: If there is a look of surprise on their face as you are delivering their annual review, you have failed in your job. Reviews should be the result of previous feedback, coaching, mentoring and even counseling. I was never surprised in a review, indicating that every boss had made it a point to do the job right all year long.

To accomplish a productive review session, it is important that employees are given time to reflect upon their performance prior to a sit down session. They need to have had ample time to assess themselves. Often, I find that they are harder on themselves. There is a question as to when to tell an employee about their raise and

"Major Opportunities"

that is debatable. I always felt like if it was great increase, give it to them right up front, it will inspire them to listen carefully, fully understanding you think they have done a great job. If it is average to below average, tell them at the end, I suspect they already may know that.

Building Block 7
"Terminations & Separations -with Dignity"

The best way I can think of to explain this building block would be with another story. It involves a store manager I had to release one year. He had been with the company for thirty-five years and he was a very nice man. He was a family man, had always been a company man but he did not manage to stay on track with the program as we changed over the year. His store was not merchandised well, his results were terrible, his theft rampant, his people were frustrated, and his turnover was high. He had received a "Needs improvement," on his annual review the previous year. At mid-year the following year, the district manager was out so I held that job for a few months. Based upon three of my visits in the first six months, continued dismal results and complaints from several employees in a roundtable I conducted, it was clear things were not improving. He was already on a written counseling from his last annual review, which was standard operating procedure when we issued a needs improvement review.

By mid-year I had no option but to rate him a, "Needs Improvement," once again. When I went to complete the mid-year review, I had another store manager traveling with me who was training to become a district manager. As part of his training, observing the final written warning of a thirty-five plus year long-standing employee over age forty was good training. I told him he was to be a fly on the wall and, "Flies do not talk," I said to him. To be fair to the store manager, I spent an inordinate amount of time selling him on the changes he must make in order to keep his job. I was still hopeful by some miracle that he might change but my gut feeling told me we might be way past that point.

Nevertheless, I did give him the David Slaughter motivational speech implying that, "You can do this!" He was shaking his head and smiling all the while. Interestingly, based upon his own self-evaluation he had completed he too was in complete agreement that he had not improved. All of the sudden when I had asked him if he understood the point I was making, his right hand shot up like a bullet and startled, I said "Yes," as if I thought he was raising his hand in a classroom to provide the answer. He said, "I believe," "I believe," he said again!" I am not sure if I should have found water and offered to baptize him and it did startle both of us in the room, it made all three of us chuckle at the same time . . . I guess my call to "Jesus session," as he saw it, had not been wasted. For the record, "To believe," means to change and real change, there would not be.

Jumping to the end of the year, the district manager was back in the saddle and the store manager did make any progress. He worked long hours; he smiled and frequently said yes sir and no ma'am on visits. As the store director, since it was a store in my territory, since I had in effect been the district manager for half the year so I could not slough my responsibility. I could not excuse myself as part of this tough decision. I made it in partnership with HR and it was that it was time to part ways. I arranged for a severance package we offered as a company. It was actually a very large severance should he choose to accept it and begin anew. It is never an easy task to terminate anyone, we all hate that part of the job but it does have to occur and it must be conducted with great respect and dignity. Strangely, we went to lunch together that day and he had requested a copy of the separation as we left the store. After lunch, we stopped at a local copy place to pick up a fax and again he reminded me he needed a copy of the review. Anytime you are separating an employee who has many years with a company, over the age of forty, there is always risk

"Major Opportunities"

in the decision, so it did perk my ears up when this usually timid individual reminded me that he wanted, needed, a copy.

As I looked up while making the copy for him he smiled and said to me, "Oh it's not for me of course, it's for my lawyer," gulp, I swallowed hard. Then he said while smiling ear to ear, "Mr. Slaughter, I'm just kidding with you, I just wanted a copy for my own records," Gotcha, the joke was on me as I thought, "This guy does have a sense of humor and he does have the heart of gold I knew him to have all along. He was a very decent man, lost in the translation of a changing retail environment. We both received a laugh out of it that afternoon, he promptly signed his severance package the next day, he moved on and we placed a new manager in the store.

Termination and separation with dignity is important and it is a major opportunity to treat people right no matter what the outcome of your employment relationship may turn out to be. If you do the right thing, it will be okay and its one of the things I respected most about Stage Stores Inc. Some companies take the easy way out on separations and terminations, especially in right to work states where they can just say goodbye but Stage Stores Inc. has always taken the high road by typically offering severances based upon length of time in position unless it involved theft or dishonesty. I always saw that as one factor that made us unique in the treatment of others with dignity and respect, by doing what is right. Sometimes, you just have to close the door but it can be handled professionally with respect and dignity towards the employee, as if you are applying the golden rule.

~ Chapter 10 ~
"Major Opportunities to Succeed"

Just because we keep referring to doors that can open or because we refer to opportunities there for the taking, does not mean that these opportunities always equate to measured successes in life. Often, the success enjoyed takes times, perseverance, patience and in the end, it usually requires a commitment to remaining on track with a written plan of action and a means of measure. In this chapter, we will explore ways to achieve a consistent level of success. We have previously examined the role of importance a strong mentor can have upon your success, both in business and in personal endeavors, now let us address our potential to succeed.

A "Vision of Success," Begins Early!

The path to success begins most often, very early in life. Many factors including; one's up-bringing, one's exposure to a good education, involvement in organized sports, even the influence of those around you independent of your immediate family can all have an impact upon an individual's ability to succeed in life. Doors of major opportunity during this time are most often doors opened by others, for you. This is certainly not a book about how to raise your children, God knows that formula is too complicated to explain and I am clearly not qualified to write that book, despite having five children. I submit that the extent to which a parent presents early life experiences to their children as opportunities to succeed or fail, to contribute to how they learn to deal with hurdles and obstacles later in life, has a huge impact upon their lifetime of successes. Those experiences, common referred to as mistakes can serve as a good barometer to learn from helping one to avoid the same mistakes that should be learned early in life. Too often, one parent or both try to shield or protect their child, a natural instinct for many. However, in being over protective they may deprive a child of access to doors that will become harder to recognize as opportunities later in life. No parent is perfect, most try the best they can, but the best advice I could offer is let them try to succeed, sometimes failing while they do it. It is better to look inside doors early on, in order to go inside and stay inside of the best ones down the road.

What makes Me Successful?

The question we must try to answer is what can makes one successful, or for that matter what is success? I would like to limit the discussion primarily to a few key factors that appear to have a significant impact upon one's successes. These include; training and education, competition they are exposed to, and the habits one forms. To begin with, a clinical definition of success according to Miriam Webster's dictionary is "degree or measure of succeeding b: favorable or desired outcome; also: the attainment of wealth, favor, or eminence." Accordingly, for the purpose of this book, this translates in the real world as to what it takes to achieve your dream in life. Everyone's dream may differ, most dream of being wealthy, some happy, many better off than their parents were. Although most of us typically measure success in financial terms, success can be measured by one's interest in helping others, in living a life where one's work is tied to their sense of pride.

Let's stay focused on achieving success through great results. For me, the single most important concern I had from the moment that I hit the sales floor back in 1983 until I received my first major promotion into management was intrinsically linked to an obsessive focus on setting goals and tracking the results closely. The only way I can provide an example of what this process includes is to simply state, one must become obsessed beyond merely a simple definition of obsessive compulsive in terms of having a desire to make your sales numbers. You must think about it all of the time, you must track it to the penny, you must not let go of the goal in your mind, ever. The top sales men or women in any field are usually obsessed with making their numbers; and they always find a way to do it. They are obsessed to the point that they might make others nauseous at the thought of seeing them most days, or at even at hearing the words that come out of their mouth. I think in large part, jealousy is rooted in an acceptance that mediocrity is what they prefer. Often misunderstood, these top producers are concerned very little with your lack of desire to be number one as they are consumed with reaching the top, usually at all costs, I know because I was one of them and I too climbed to the top. Most people have a potential to make it to the top but it takes desire, hard work and a constant willingness to raise your goals in order to continue to raise the bar of success.

Goal setting & Means of Measure

To obtain success in any endeavor you undertake you must set goals. In terms of specific goal setting, I personally set much higher goals than most due to the structure of competition that I was exposed to in competitive debate and through my sport experiences. The fact remains that too often people set goals that are either too low or too high, rarely, just right. Either of those ways of setting a goal guarantees not being as successful as one might be. When goals are set low, it gives a false sense of what is good, or what the standard of good is. The standard for sales achievement should be considered a "good" result, not average or below average. On the other hand, if the goals are set too high, there tends to be an acceptance that the goals are just too high resulting in complacency as one accepts their inability to achieve the goal. Consequently, they never reach the top or maximize a stretch goal. At Stage Stores Inc., we always made sure the standard for our stores would satisfy that they were doing a good job that as a requirement of being a good employee was what was required of them, that good is good, not average.

I have always been obsessed with writing my goals down and then tracking them, by the hour, by the day, by the month and by the year. When you are obsessed with your numbers and goals at that level, you do develop an ability to walk into most any retail store, much less one of your own 200 stores, quickly able to predict the volume that store might be against for the day within a few cents. It just takes crunching numbers as a living, setting goals repeatedly and hitting them. The simple lesson for you is dig into the goals, set what you want as a goal, set one that allows you to feel rewarded and then keep rising and hitting the goals, it is fun to win.

Tracking forms, daily sales cards, have become a discontinued practice among some companies due to the elimination of most commission programs. However, I totally disagree with these tools becoming extinct. In this competitive world, now, more than ever companies should utilize in some format or another a tool that holds employees accountable for their results and those sales goals should be tied into a non-negotiable aspect that defines that they are doing a good job. When people are accountable for their results, they tend to produce more. I challenge any executive or manager to prove me wrong as history and empirical data is on my side.

Becoming obsessed with numbers!

For most retailers, for those of us who rely upon sales numbers and sales goals to manage and measure success, the number one opportunity to succeed is for everyone to know the number and to become obsessed with making it! Having achieved a high level of sales improvement in every position that I held over those years, I will explain how I did it. I was obsessed with knowing the number we were against, ask anyone. In every role I served, simply by knowing the number, by insisting on everyone in management know the number, we generally always made the number. It was as simple as all of us moving towards the goal as a as a team, every-day.

The truth of it is, most retailers get caught up in the operations, the memos, the freight work, chasing shoplifters, customer complaints, personnel issues, phone calls, paperwork, and drama in general. They spent entirely too much time in their office when they should be on the floor making it happen. Now do me a favor just as a simple exercise, take a piece of paper management team member, store manager, or district manager and write down all of the reasons why you are not out on the floor in the midst of things driving towards the number once your store is open. Now do me a favor, take that piece of paper with all of those excuses and go give it to someone who cares, because I do not. Your major opportunity, your door that needs to be opened relies upon an acceptance that you have to become more obsessed with the numbers, how to meet and exceed the number every day, every week, every month, period. They are all just excuses for why you are letting most of the things that interfere with your ultimate goal take precedence over the one and one thing that really matters, comp sales.

Now I do understand from having run two ten million dollar stores and a sixty million dollar district, a hundred and twenty million region and a four hundred fifty million territory that all of that operational stuff does have to be done. I understand there is a lot to accomplish but you do that by delegating and following up, by doing it with them, by teaching and training, by hiring and maintaining great people, by creating a great atmosphere, by making it fun and in general by holding people accountable. In the mean-time, let me provide you with a story of an exercise

"Major Opportunities"

I did with my 200 store managers in an effort to drive home the point that we have to know our numbers, move towards them as the one and only real objective to get through that door of success.

One of my responsibilities twice a year was to prepare the agenda, the materials for our bi-annual store manager meetings. Pat was responsible for the same with the district manager meetings and we both worked on each of them in an effort to tie it all together. After the district manager meetings, usually in Houston, we would all head out into the field to participate in as many of the 28 store managers meetings as was physically possible. This particular set of meetings we talked a great deal about the subject I have given you, driving sales, making the number, how to improve sales. Although we discussed many ways to achieve that including, merchandise to affect sales, developing top sales persons, opening charge accounts to gain repeat business and focusing upon key hours of the day where store traffic was the highest. The most important item we began each meeting with centered upon knowing your numbers.

I went to a toy store and bought a remote control red "Stuart Little" sports car just like the one he drove around in the kids movie I had seen with my daughters, three times. It was fun to play with in advance of taking it with me on the road to all of my meetings but the purpose behind it was so much larger and so much more fun. Prior to each meeting whether it was in a large store back room or a hotel, I would tape a yellow x on one side of the room and another one on the opposite corner of the room. At the beginning of each meeting as I kicked off our meetings that the district managers would actually conduct that day, I began by saying that today we are going to talk about the most important major opportunity we have this year, to drive sales. I told them I wanted to start by having some fun. I asked all of them to get up and come with me to the back of the room. I asked for two volunteers, which I always received almost immediately.

I put "Stuart little" in his cute little red car on the floor and showed them how much fun it was to play with as several of my children already knew as well. Then I told one of the volunteers that I wanted him or she to drive the car from the one marked off spot we were standing next to across the room to the other spot marked home. They quickly said, "No problem, I can do that." Before handing them my prized little toy car, I responded by saying the following, "Oh I forgot to tell you, you have to wear this blindfold but the other volunteer can help you by calling out instructions for you to follow in an effort to get there quickly as you can, I am sure you will do just fine." Then they were blindfolded and the real fun began. You might be able to imagine what was to follow. Instructions from the helper included comments like, "Okay go to the left, no turn to the left, no go back, no, no, no, just stop, stop touching the controller. Let's just start over," the helper would say in the first minute or so of the activity. Of course, the person that was driving was blind so they really did not even know where they were, where they were going or how to get there, as they had no plan for the trip. After four or five minutes the Stuart little car was stuck, it was upside down, or under a table, never close to the final destination and there was frustration in the communication between the driver and the helper. I told the driver they could now remove the blind fold and they could try it by themselves now being able to see where they needed to go and seeing the right path their car needed to take to go straight there. Amazingly, they all easily drove directly to that designated spot and often with a sigh of relief in front of their own peers as they parked Mr. Stuart Little on the X marked home sweet home.

With little lights seemingly coming on in their minds early in the meeting, I asked them to all sit back down to resume our meeting. The first thing I asked the group was, "Was that fun?" They all said yes except for the driver and now with my icebreaker effectively accomplished, I explained the following. I said to them, "When you get in your car to go somewhere, isn't it easier to arrive on time when you know where you are going?" I asked the entire group "Isn't this exactly the same as it is with making your sales number each day?" "Don't you have to know where you are going, don't you have to know the number, without that information, without having a way to see it, and aren't you limiting your ability to ever get there if you do not?" By now, lights were coming on throughout the room, knowing they now probably felt set-up I said, "Ladies and gentlemen, it is time for us to commit to knowing numbers each day of the year, it is time to obsess over making our numbers, it is time to insist that our management teams know the number." "Most importantly," I said, "Isn't it time for us to spend this day talking about specific actionable ways to drive Stuart Little to that designated spot called home or in our case, called our sales goal?" Lights visibly on now, they all understood the direction that I wanted to go, we now had a map in our hands and together, we had a full day of planning how to open those doors in order to achieve the major opportunities that were ahead. You and your leaders must set the pace as the ones that become obsessed with knowing the goals, staying focused with the goal in mind as the top priority each day and you too will climb to the top more consistently.

Finding Balance in life—in the Middle!

One of the things that many of us struggle within life, especially those of us top guns, is how to find the a way to strike a healthy balance between a pursuit of measurable career objectives while finding a way to maintain some sense of sanity and normality in one's personal life. This is no easy task to accomplish with even the best of intentions. I have watched as we do it by having more children, I have personally validated that bigger cars, bigger homes and material possessions are an attempt to reward ourselves for putting in too much time at work. I have learned through personal experience and reflection that despite how nice it is to have material things to enjoy, it is the balance between work and personal time that seems ultimately to be the most rewarding. Having said that, it is my hope you will find this balance much earlier in your life than I did. That balance can take the form of a hobby, reading, just getting out and forgetting the pressures of work on a consistent basis. Personally, I have found some balance in jogging at Memorial park, in Houston. That six mile jog, walk or run around the course offers time to clear my head, and many words recorded in this book were written in my head running on that trail several times a week. Each individual must determine the best way to maintain a healthy balance as it varies significantly between two individuals.

The term balance, defined in the Miriam Webster dictionary was that I find useful as; 2: a means of judging or deciding, 3: a counterbalancing weight, force, or influence. These two definitions provide a good basis for thought. One can effectively utilize their personal life as a natural, healthy way to offset those pressures of the drive for success, even for survival in one's business life. Moreover, a counterbalance of distraction can offer escape from those pressures as well. I often heard throughout my life, you have to find a hobby. Not always true, one just has to find their solace or inner peace that offers respite from the rigors and pressures of everyday life. One of the most effective ways to achieve a healthy balance between work and your personal life, as a method to remain sane among the most aggressive, motivated, folks like you and me is called a "bucket list."

When I was thirty-five years old, I wrote down one hundred things I wanted to accomplish by the time I was fifty. In the final tabulation, I accomplished ninety-eight of them. The only two I missed include; go to Paris and run a marathon. The marathon story I have already shared in this book with you already and the Paris story, but let us just say my ex-wife's new husband took her to Paris and asked for her hand in marriage, which she of course, accepted. Having let go of that secret for all of you, I have to say that she is a wonderful mother of my five children and is still a good friend, but now at least you understand my personal Paris failure. Interestingly, my failure, turned out to become his success. No matter what, ninety-eight out of one hundred is a high mark on any test so I am ok with that score. Although some of the items were silly, even some being mundane, I did attempt to strike a good balance between career accomplishments over those fifteen years and personal achievements. I recently made a new list at the ripe old age of fifty including twenty-five items to accomplish by my 60th birthday. I will share a few of those with you the following:

1) Publish a book
2) Find the woman that I will spend the rest of my life with
3) Complete a research project for the Kettering Foundation
4) Raise a million dollars for charity in one year
5) Complete my Masters in Non-profit management
6) Take non-profit classes at Rice University
7) Form a 5013c non-profit charity
8) Make contact with three old friends from high school
9) Make contact with my lost and forgotten older brother
10) Learn to play the piano

The other bucket list items are somewhere in a vault!

Preparing a "Bucket list" is a healthy exercise as one pursues their "Major Opportunities." I encourage you to put the book down for a moment and write down five items as you begin your own bucket list. I too sat down with my youngest, Ellie and she came up with 10-bucket list items for her and I to complete over the next 365 days. Initially her list had us taking five trips around the world (she is 10) and I told her she gets one trip in 365 days. She also included; pet an Ostrich, hit a double in softball, swim with dolphins and sing at Barnes and Noble. Perhaps a book signing at Barnes and Noble can occur someday soon. No matter what, I know we will have fun over these next twelve months as father and daughter as we create memories together, perhaps even begin a tradition for the two of us. As a side note, I found it interesting, actually cute that one of her ten items included getting one specific teacher for fifth grade next year. I did inquire on her behalf and I believe she is in line have her after all. She must be very special, "I will see what I can do," I told her.

I want to hear about your success stories and about your bucket list. Who knows, there may just be a book entitled "Filling the Bucket Full," so start your list today. Another name for your bucket list can be of course, "Major Opportunities." Remember through, put many items into your list that are for personal achievement. Avoid filling your bucket with only career successes as most often I have determined through personal experience that is usually, "Half-full."

So now, go fill your bucket with FUN!

~ Chapter 11 ~

"Getting Them to Come Back, By Getting Them to Stay"

Occasionally, someone will ask me if I know of a magical formula for success. The response I always give is the same, "Yes, I do." As I begin to explain, sometimes they listen and sometimes they do not. You did not ask that question of me but you did buy this book so I want to make my answer available to you by providing the formula, then of course, my secret will be yours. It is the one proven method one can rely upon in order to stay on top of Mount Success." It is a magic formula, guaranteeing success for any company at the highest level and it is as simple as the title of this chapter, "Getting them to come back, by getting them to stay."

When I say "Getting them to come back," I am referring to the customer, getting them, your customer to come back in is what really matters, isn't it? I would be less than honest if I did not say, it is all that matters because it is the one way you can guarantee future sales, future business, and it is the single best way to create and maintain your unique "Brand" necessary for survival. A "Brand" must be able to survive issues in the economy, competition or natural changes, adjustments, and fluctuations in business. When I complete the statement, "By getting them to stay," I refer to getting your employees to stay with you by to continue working for you. I am referring to the basic essentials for success that we have previously examined including; consistently maintaining low turnover, maintaining a higher than industry average of seasoned experienced employees on your team, and relying upon a well-trained, motivated, happy team to keep you on top. Getting them to come back, referring to the customer occurs by getting them, the employees, to stay.

I can illustrate my premise by relying upon one of the best retail examples of which I am aware in 2013. This story, this company and this model demonstrate success in the real world. This model is a company I have personally relied upon for nineteen years as a customer. In my opinion, being responsible for 14 districts, 200 stores and 3500 employees, the company, "Visible Changes," epitomizes how to employ a business strategy by making it fun. It provides a second model for you of a retailer who understands how to rely upon their people and a strong business formula to succeed. In my mind, they reflect a company that proves through consistent results how important it still is to become and to remain a strong brand name over an extended time without losing their identity.

According to information from their web site, in 1977, Visible Changes began a revolution in the hairdressing industry with a company that delivered quality services from well-trained stylists. John and Maryanne McCormack began with one salon in in Houston, Texas. The company has grown to include 17 salons across the state of Texas. Today, Visible Changes has hair salons located in major malls in Houston, Austin, San Antonio and Plano (Dallas area). They just celebrated thirty-five years as a company and interestingly, as I dug deeper, I discovered that recently they were as the number one place to work as an employee, in the 4th largest city in the US, named by Houston Business Journal's as the "Best Places to Work 2012."

Those two facts alone warrant high honor, merit special recognition, and justifies additional study and deserves copying. I can speak emphatically to nineteen of those thirty-five years they celebrated as a loyal customer. As one might imagine, having been in retail myself for twenty-four years, having done it from the ground up as a sales associate occupying a role in upper management, I understand their success. Therefore, I suspect you can understand why I go back each time.

Let's look at how both parts of that chapter title tie together represented by my own personal Visible Changes experiences. First, the getting them back part of the sentence, the customer that is. I can speak to that as an expert when it comes to this thirty five year old company. They get me back because in the nineteen plus years, I have been going into their location in Sugarland Mall but also in the Houston Galleria, I have never had one single incident where I ever felt miss-treated, or taken for granted.

Understanding retail as it is, through some first-hand in the trench experience as a store manager, a district manager and a store director, I happen to know that negative situations in daily customer contact do happen. I also understand that misunderstandings do occur, that mistakes are made and, I understand it is not a perfect world and not all employees are perfect either. However, for that matter we customers can be having a bad day too, we may not be so perfect ourselves. However, remember my new friends, the customer is always the boss, and the customer is always right, we do remember that caveat, right?

Having stated that, I have never once heard an unhappy customer while being inside any of their locations, period. Now I am sure the store managers, even the district managers have plenty of stories to share in private. When you never hear it or see once in nineteen years and you are a guy who listens for and sees every detail around him, with spock-like ears, with eyes in the back of his head, it means either it is unusual that it occurs or that it is handled so quietly or so professionally that it seems as if it is not there. Either way, it gets lost in great service and that secret revealed alone separates Visible Changes from their industry, from their malls, from their competition, and for the purposes of this example, it puts them on a pedestal that cannot go unnoticed or ignored.

Third, I personally keep on coming back because it is consistent. It is consistently clean, it is consistently well lit, it is consistently decorated throughout the year with different, always relevant themes and it is a consistently a fun place to visit. Coincidently, it is consistently full of customers. It is fun in the sense that from the minute you are greeted at the front counter until you check out again as you leave, you are treated with smiles, with courtesy, in a way that makes you feel special, NEVER with an attitude, ALWAYS with a solution, not an excuse. The music is fun, the place is always buzzing and it is a place that systematically relaxes and soothes you while they are focused on your every need including; water, comfort, magazines, while all along being sensitive to your time, that most precious commodity.

The second part of that sentence in the title of this chapter, "By getting them to stay," referring to employees, is important to their success by sharing the main reason I keep coming back. The reason I keep coming back is due to the fact they do such a great job getting their employees to stay on as employees. For many years now, one of their key people, Thi has been my one and only choice for hair care. Thi has been cutting my hair in the Sugarland Mall location for seventeen years and Elennys has been taking the grey out of my sideburns for four or five years now. No one else but Thi will ever cut my hair if I can help it and no one but Elennys will ever put any color in my hair. For that matter, no one is even supposed to find out that I get rid of the grey, but now you know, but you women do it too, so let's not go there.

Thi and Elennys remain the single most important reason for me to continue coming back to Visible Changes, as they are incredible employees. The fact remains, because they both keep staying there as happy, loyal, rewarded employees, I keep coming back as their customer, as a Visible Changes customer. They make me look better, they make me feel better, and they make me better.

I have never had a bad haircut from Thi, only great ones, in fact I always feel better than when I walked in to see either of them. Always treated as a priority, they make me feel special, as a team. They never fight over their share of the products I buy, they share the credit, and they share the results. They never pry into my personal life, but we can all admit that for some reason or another often we are excessively willing to spill our guts to the person that cuts or colors our hair, they could probably write a book themselves. In this case, Thi and Elennys are my friends and I come back because they choose to stay. If they are on vacation, I will wait.

What Thi and Elennys do not know is that this chapter was written so many weeks ago and then, after avoiding them so as to avoid a haircut in my on-going rebellious time (I like my hair longer), I purposely went into the store in early January and let them do their thing, finally. They worked as a team and two hours later, $200 later, I left ready for my photo shoot for the back cover of this book, which I never told them during the two hours was the real reason I was there. So when you see me on the front cover of this book, see them!

Now, for the record, their professional services do not come at that high of a price. It was the four other products that without high pressure, I left with in order to insure that my hair is healthy. I was not there to spy on anyone. I have accomplished that for fifteen years every few months when I frequented their store. I was not there to write this story as, it had been written over these many years of great customer service. This day in January, I only confirmed what I already knew, that they both love what they do, they love their customers, they love their company and for me, they define the Visible Changes vision of success.

"Getting them to come back is clear but what about the second half of the equation, "by getting them to stay?" Well, I figured out that their employees keep on staying due to several factors. Factors based upon research as a customer and based upon interviews over the years with employees. You must suspect by now that I talk, and I do. You may have figured out I ask questions, and I do but what you need to know is that in every case I asked an employee at Visible Changes why they have worked there so long, they usually give me the exact same response. They tell me they stay because it is fun, because they are treated well and because they have good benefits.

So let me get this right, I too go back because it is fun, because I get treated well and because of the benefits to me personally and I keep going back over and over again mainly, because they (the employees), keep staying there to work. What a formula for guaranteed success, the secret is now out. It is no wonder they were named as the best place to work in Houston in 2012 and it is no wonder they just celebrated thirty-five years of success as a company. I bet they have thirty-five more good years coming.

We need to explore the final piece of the puzzle explaining why they keep on staying as employees with this unique company. I know because I asked them repeatedly over the years, mainly because it was often the same employees I saw each time I went into a store. According to many of them, it is because Visible Changes rewards their employees with positive reinforcement including daily praise and recognition, they still allow for trips to be taken by management and by specialist to travel to fun places, while they focus upon training. It is because they still reward top achievers with awards that they can remember, like trips, trophies and other items; loyal employees told me. It is because over the years, despite good economic times and bad, they have stayed the course of rewarding with purpose, not just in speech or promises undelivered. That fact separates them from the rest of their competition.

This chapter would have not been complete had I not accepted an invitation to attend the yearly Visible Changes awards banquet at the Hilton of the Americas here in Houston in March, 2013. Something told me that it was worth getting dressed up for and I surprised my stylist Thi, but Elennys was in on it all along. I sat with the group from First Colony in Sugarland and it felt as though I was with family. I met owner John McCormack Senior for the first time and of course, he was right in the middle of the action, greeting all of his beloved employees and friends.

The event was one of the most exciting events I have attended in years. The fashion show was like something out of Cirque de

"Major Opportunities"

Soleil as the only way to describe the atmosphere would be to use the words energetic, electric, exciting, and enthusiastic. I confirmed that this company cares deeply about their employee and they care about rewarding them with praise, prizes trips and cars, yes—even cars. There were ten cars sitting out front in the lobby with bows on them, all given away that very day based upon a raffle where an employee had their name placed in the drawing according to their results.

Visible Changes recognizes success at all levels. There was an award for the graduating class of 2012, the new folks that had survived, those that would become the future of Visible Changes. There were many service awards including 5, 10, 20, and 30 years. There were awards for sales and right in the middle of it all was the president, the son, Johnny. He did not treat them as employees he treated them as family. I understand why so many employees had told me that it is like being in one big family. It was an event that I will remember the rest of my life and I hope I am invited back next year. I left there feeling the way I describes for you in Chapter one, it was a great day, it was a day that super bowls should be played on. I have no clue how much this event cost the owners but I suspect they understand that you have to spend money to make money and I can honestly say that I have NEER seen such excitement in a meeting in my 55 years on this planet, it was a first class event from start to finish.

The Visible Changes "culture" is not limited to just having a good team or to producing positive results in just one store. Since moving from Sugarland to inside the loop over ten years ago, I would not be honest with you if I did not say that I do frequent the Houston Galleria Visible Changes out of convenience sometimes. I always preached passionately to my stores, especially to my district managers that you have to have a back-up plan. I prefer an A, a B, and a C if possible. Although you hope you never have to use the C, you often must go with a B if the A does not work out.

I am referring of course to staffing, promotions and replacement of employees. What I know to be true is that with the Sugarland store and the Galleria store in mind, I have two A's and that is a good plan. Specifically, there is Jamie, the store manager in the Galleria location. I occasionally interrupt Jamie when I am in the Galleria to inquire about some new product or a new opportunity to do what I like to call some "me-search or perhaps to just get a conditioner in between cuts." I have learned to trust his opinions, he has never been wrong. In this high volume store, high traffic mall environment Jamie always stops and takes the time he needs to talk with me. Setting aside the fact that it's nice to see the same manager in a store repeatedly, more importantly it's nice to see one that is always there, always in the thick of the action. It was nice to see him one of the key people calling off winners of awards. Clearly, the company places great emphasis on involving their key people, as Jamie had a key role throughout the event.

Recently, I went into the Houston Galleria store with the notion that a different type conditioner was necessary. I waited for Jamie to have a moment to visit with me and as we were talking, he introduced me to another incredible employee, Katrina, "Like the hurricane," she said. What I observed on this particular visit was the way that Jamie collaborated with Katrina concerning what treatment to recommend, as a way to gain her professional opinion; they actually touched my hair to feel the texture. In my research mode always, in passing, I asked Jamie how long he had been with Visible Changes, he said sixteen years here and twenty-one in total but he deflected the attention away from himself and said, "But Katrina has me beat." She then told me she has been there twenty-two years and that she works some in the corporate office as well as the store. As we talked, mainly me of course, I asked her why she has stayed with the company so long and she said it was because of the owners, "I love them," she said, "They are the best." I was Katrina's customer that day, she stayed with me until I was finished and yes I bought three more products in my "me-search" mode of research but please don't tell Thi or Elennys, for now let's keep this our dirty little secret.

Mainly that day in the Houston galleria location, I confirmed again that Visible Changes is a great company because the employees love their company, their owners and they love their job, so they stay as employees and I come back as their customer. As I checked out with a young woman at the counter that day, I asked her how long she had been there. She said over four years now. I said, "What do you like about your job." She responded with, "Well, it's like being part of a big family." Interestingly, when I went home that night I read a business journal article which clarified why she sees it that way, it's because they want it that way as I read, "We try to keep a strong family culture and keep it consistent throughout the salons," said President John W. McCormack. Culture and leadership starts from the top and trickles down and John McCormack obviously practices what he preaches, the employees see it, hear it and they feel it. Convinced my research was now complete, knowing I needed to close this chapter of the book, I left the Galleria salon that day knowing that having two great choices is always better than having an A and a B, but my heart still belongs to Thi and Elennys, just for the record.

I had to ask myself, where do all these loyal employees get their knowledge? I found the answer it is because they train them. According to a Houston Business Journal article, "Visible Changes has a six- to 18 month training program to teach the fundamentals of color chemical mixing and hair-cutting techniques." One of the biggest things we focus on is the education that we provide for our staff," the younger McCormack said. "We believe if you don't, you are doomed to mediocrity. Education is the only way to break through barriers and become extraordinary."

At the awards event it was interesting and inspiring to see that they gave an award to the owner of Guadalajara Restaurants for him making his parking lot available for employees that come downtown to train. I think they said on his award, that without him, these employees could not have received their training and the entire crowd of 1200 applauded.

In today's competitive retail world, in a world where is has become commonplace for companies to cut payroll year after year, commonplace to continue cutting budgets, continue to eliminate meetings, conferences and seminars, Visible Changes still stands tall. In a world where companies team two employees together in a hotel room in order to minimize expenses, where giving awards, trips and trophies as prizes has become seemingly outdated, Visible Changes still refuses to budge. I find it interesting, refreshing and inspiring that Visible Changes still employs these incredibly motivational tools and rewards. They are always rated highly every single year and they just keep growing and growing. The owners at Visible Changes seem to understand that it takes money to make money. It takes putting your money where your mouth is, and that they do.

I found out that Visible Changes does not just give to their customers; they give back to the community. According to the company's President, John McCormack, "Twenty years ago, the company established the Visible Changes Educational Foundation. Since then, it has put thirty graduates through the program, all children of Visible Changes employees." "If one of the children of our employees needs help, the scholarship foundation is there to help them improve," he said. Eighty percent of the foundation is geared toward college students, but it also extends out to high school students and helps with tutoring services." "Education is what separates people, what we believe in," he said, "whether it be in hairdressing or in life. People who have a better shot in life tend to be more educated. We have made a commitment to our stylists, as well as our children. Hopefully, it trickles back into our community" So when I wrote in another chapter that there are "Major Opportunities" to pass it on, Visible Changes philosophy provides proof of that and as have I told you previously, when you pass it on, it usually always comes back to you.

I have now provided you with two great models including my old company and the Visible Changes model. Your company too can model this formula for success. It is not contained in any company Performa or spreadsheet, it is not about firing everybody and starting all over again, it is not about finding one new highly recruited sought after employee, it is not even linked to a new manager or a new district manager. Instead, it is affected and

"Major Opportunities"

it often the result of the atmosphere you create in your place of business. It will depend almost completely on how you treat your people, how much fun you make it to come to work, and how you consistently you reward them and praise them for their effort.

Now despite what you may read into this chapter, I am clearly not their paid spokes men, there is no free haircut or benefit coming, even though I could be a nioxin sales clerk, without a doubt. With some encouragement, I was compelled to step off the Stage Stores Inc. band-wagon for a moment. Even though I proudly told you how we did it, I wanted to provide you with another successful company as another model to examine, providing you testimony that it is happening elsewhere in the retail world. I wanted you to know that you and your company can accomplish it as well.

While preparing this final manuscript for what seemed like the twelve hundredth time as I shared this Visible Changes model with a close friend, she asked if I had shared any of this good news with Visible Changes themselves. It was a good question. I decided to contact my Sugarland store and I talked with the manger Rosanna who was pleased to hear how great my experiences have been over the years. She provided a name and a number for me to call so I could share my story with someone at the top of the company. I called the number at the corporate office and a young woman answered by the name of Crystal. I told her I needed to talk to the person that was highest up that she could locate, that I had a story to share. I did not say whether it was a good-bad story or a Good-Great story. Now, I know from first-hand experience that usually it is the negative information or complaints that cause someone to insist on speaking to someone high-up. In addition, knowing as I do that it is usually one of the jobs of the person on the other end of the phone to fend off those trauma-producing calls, or perhaps to try to diffuse them prior to them getting all the way to the top.

Remarkably, instead of sloughing me off or transferring me somewhere else, Crystal said the following to me, "Well Mr. Slaughter, I know just what to do. Can you hold on and I will be right back, don't go anywhere," were her instructions to me. Momentarily she came back on the line and said she was going to transfer me to Carl Fairman, she said he has been with the company for many years and that he is one she "picked" for me to talk to. Carl and I had a pleasant conversation, we committed to meeting face to face, and we briefly discussed the possibility of my attending the company meeting at the Hilton in March as a guest, which I did get the opportunity to do.

I got off the phone and thought to myself, this story is not just about one person, one success story or even just one positive experience; it is about a company success, it is a great story about a "Company brand." A great company is a great brand represented by everyone in the organization from the top to the bottom, from the newest employee to the most senior employee, from Crystal to the owner.

Interestingly, as I was visiting with a dean of University of Houston-Downtown, Dr. Christina Birchak she offered some positive feedback to complete my research. She is a wise, highly educated woman and as I shared this latest chapter, she informed me that she too has been one of their customers now for over sixteen years. Without giving me even an opportunity to ask, she said, "Do you know why I have been going there for sixteen years David?" She said her take on why she has continued to go back is because she thinks of them as a company, "Where they always remember your name." That sounded to me like a "Cheers" bar song to me or some commercial playing somewhere in my head. As she told me this story I was reminded of how many times over the years I have called to make an appointment or to make a change, only to hear the employee at the other end of the phone speak my name. I suspect my dean's hair specialist has been there a long time too and my guess is that she keeps on going back, because her stylist chooses to stay.

So what's in a name, you ask? Well, everything is in a name as it can become the "brand" for a moment or it can become a "brand" for thirty-five years like it has at Visible Changes or it just may just become a "Brand" for a lifetime. An established brand

"Major Opportunities"

name supported by employees who are loyal to that brand, is the main reason customers keep coming back for more. For you see, "Getting them to come back, by getting them to stay," is the Visible Changes WAY!

~ *Chapter 12* ~
"Major Opportunities," to Pass It On"

"Major Opportunities" in life are not just there for the taking, there are also some revolving doors of opportunity that offer one a chance to give back to the world. As we consider the many ways in life to pass it on, I begin with one simple rule and it is, "treat people right." How many times have you seen an issue occur between people because of the way they talked to one another or acted towards another person? I insisted to my employees that speaking to every single customer defined their job. Speaking to others when you pass them or you just catch a glimpse of them, is so very basic to being a human on this planet . . . A simple rule to employ when you pass another fellow human is you speak. If you miss that opportunity, you may not be human. If you prefer just to keep it simple, simply say, "Hello fellow human." A smile is good, a nod of the head is better, a shake of a hand is nice, or a "how do you do?" will suffice. One cannot take these basic common courtesies for granted, yet I see it done every single day of my life. Whatever method you employ in greeting, it is common courtesy to speak, period. How you treat others in life will often determine how you are treated. Treat people nice and good things will follow, often they will smile back.

Treating people right

As opportunities come and go both in our professional and in our personal life experiences, I have determined that there are occasions presented that allow a potential to pass it on. The term passing it on can offer a wide range of "Major Opportunities" including; the giving of your time, assisting with a needy cause, perhaps providing financial resources so that others can direct useful funds to the right place, maybe going out of your way to notice someone in need, and many others that you may have done. Passing it on can take the form of just being observant of someone around you that might need assistance, even, just by opening a door. No matter what the opportunity, looking for and providing help to others in need is the right thing to do. In my personal experience, when you pass it on by doing something good, it generally always comes back as more.

It always comes back to you!

I want to begin with a story that proves my point. I am not embarrassed to admit it but this "metrosexual" man does indeed get a manicure as often as it is allowed and I have concluded through personal experience that the second next best thing to a manicure, is a pedicure. After I resigned in 2007, I had some time on my hands, no pun intended, and easily might end up at Candy's Nails once a week for some grooming. I would like to interject at this point, to you guys that are reading this, perhaps cringing at the thought of what I am admitting to the world, well it is possible men, that you just don't get it. Grooming is essential to enjoying a complete and total life.

Second, I was one that for many years, like a moron, who would bite his nails, sometimes to the quick. Call it a bad habit, call it a nervous habit, you can call it bowing to the pressures of making the important decisions of life and in business. A manicure was my little reward for discontinuing that bad habit as well as a constant reminder not to bite. I know you women get it, you figured that one out long before Adam was chasing you around the Garden of Eden, telling you to stop spending so much money!

Having said all of that, on one particular trip into the nail salon, typically on a Saturday with one of my daughters at my side, something interesting happened. As Ellie and I stepped out of my car, looking down, I spotted a large diamond ring on the ground. Ellie saw it too and her comment to me was something like, "Daddy, can I keep it?" My response quickly was, "No, sweetie, I think that's somebody's wedding ring, let's turn it in, maybe someone will want it back." We went inside and I gave the ring to my friend Cindy, the owner of Candy's Nails. She looked somewhat surprised and then quickly rushed to put it away as a squirrel might hide a nut, thanking me for being honest. This entire time, my little five-year old Ellie kept looking at me as if I had perhaps denied her a first chance at an engagement ring, possibly even depriving her of a future with a man. "Not so fast little Ellie," I thought to myself, "Your time will come, in about a thousand years and he WILL NOT ever be good enough for you, not ever!"

I did not think about it again until some two weeks later when I went back by myself for, of course, a follow up manicure. Immediately upon entering the salon, Cindy explained to me that a woman had come in and had inquired if anyone had turned in a diamond ring. Cindy recounted that she suspiciously questioned her as to a proper description and upon realizing it was indeed the lady's ring, she pulled it out of the hidden hole she had put it in and gave it to her. Cindy explained to me that she was over-come with emotion. Cindy told her the story of my finding it and the woman asked how to contact me so that she could thank me. Cindy happened to have one of my business cards and gave it to the woman as she left with Ellie's engagement ring.

I received a call from the woman several days later and she said the following to me, "David, I wanted to tell you how much it means to me to get my wedding ring back. I suspect you may not completely understand the significance of getting something like that back, other than the sentimental value, but I wanted to let you know the situation." "You see, I have been battling a deep depression for the last few years, a clinical depression." She continued, "When I lost my wedding ring that day, knowing what I have put my poor husband through, I thought perhaps it just might be the final straw. "Instead, "she said, "My sweet little husband, hugged me, said he loved me with or without the ring, and he said it was going to be okay, everything was going to be just okay." She continued to explain as I swallowed the lump in my throat, "He said to me, it is not the ring that defines my love for you. Ring or no ring, we will be together the rest of our lives, I love you, I always have."

With her voice cracking and a tear now on my cheek, she said, "In my battle with this dark depressed state of mind that very moment moved me in the direction my doctor had been so desperately working to do. The fact that my husband loved me the same way as he did when we had married some twenty eight years before, helped me to understand the depth of our love, of his undying patience with me, and of his commitment to spend the rest of his days with me." She emotionally stated, "I am not completely finished with my battle yet, but I know now David, I can win this battle and that my priorities and my focus is to move forward, accepting that life is good, no matter what comes your way. I am doing better now and from the bottom of my heart, I thank you, you will never know what it meant to get my precious ring back."

Now, that might be the longest time in my life I have shut up and listened without interrupting someone. What she does not know was that I myself was now wiping that tear off my cheek. Swallowing slowly, I told her she had made my day and that my little Ellie, as disappointed as she might have appeared to be that she was not engaged, would be pleased to know that doing the right thing could be so very right. She asked for my address, she wanted to drop me a thank you card in the mail. I went back to what I was doing; knowing now that "Major Opportunities" do come along in life to pass it on and a good moment, can make for a great day.

The story is not over though, a few days later, I did receive a card, but it was from her, it was from her husband. He simply stated in the card, "Mr. Slaughter, you will never know what your honesty, kindness and integrity have accomplished in my life. Thank you for being honest, please accept these gift cards as a small reward, I wish it could be more, and God bless you." In the thank you card was $200 worth of assorted gift cards. I took two of them and gave them to Cindy, for you see, she too had a choice as to what to do with that precious ring. She chose to pass it on as well and when you pass it on, it usually always comes back as more. I saved one gift card for Ellie; I wanted her to receive a reward for her quick acceptance at age five, that in life, it is not just "Finders, keepers and losers, weepers." I do not recall what she bought with it, but I know it is a story we shared that neither of us will soon forget. As I read this story to her today, she smiled like an angel as if it was yesterday, she has not forgotten, I hope she never will. She is now ten and I still refuse to accept that an engagement will ever be a reality for her, my fifth of five children. The Candy's Nails ring story is not unlike what my boss Ernie Cruse tried to teach us as we ran a large company when he said, "Always do what is right and you cannot go wrong and when you do things that feel good to others, you feel good as well."

When I was ten years old, I remember hearing a preacher at one of our gospel meetings that I attended at West University Church of Christ, here in Houston. He told a very simple story in his sermon, not unlike the one I just recounted for you; it is a story that has stuck with me through all of these years. He told of getting ready to leave the church office to go home one evening and he noticed a little boy sitting by the church curb next to his bike, sobbing. He went over and asked the little boy what was wrong. The boy wiped away his tears and choking on his words he told the preacher that his dad was going to beat him when he got home. He said he had been given money to go to the store and he was to bring home bread, milk and his father's favorite cigarettes. He said, "I thought I had the money but it must have fallen out of my pocket, I just can't find it and I am getting ready to get a beating when I get home, he's gonna be mad again." James said he looked at the little boy, put an arm of support around him and told him, "Don't worry son, I will replace your lost money, your Dad will never have to know." The preacher gave the boy the money, the boy smiled as if life was now going to be okay. As the boy left, James said he sat there in his car for a moment, feeling like he had just saved a life and then the preacher told the crowd that he felt so good that he decided to drive around for a while just looking for another little boy, perhaps sitting on a curb, waiting for help as well. When you do something that is so right, it usually always comes back I have discovered. No matter what, it leaves you with a feeling in your heart of doing something good, and that, my friends, is a good thing.

Do they really even have a name?

One more story comes to mind. I think we must all struggle at one time or another with panhandlers, I know I do. Do we help them? Do we look the other way? Does it just depend on our mood or whether the guilt over takes us? Do we act as if we are on our cell phone instead of looking into their tired, old eyes? Do we help only when our children can see it or when they ask for it? My story does not really involve a panhandler on the street, but it does involve someone asking for something for nothing. What is the difference, really? They don't even have a name do they? We all hate being hit on for money we earned. Last year, I was at the university, headed to the library and another student stopped me and asked me to borrow a dollar. He said he wanted to buy a coke. I looked at him and I said, "Yes, I will be glad to give you a dollar." He thanked me and I thought nothing more about it. Months later during finals week, that same student saw me heading towards the food court, stopping me, he said, "Do you remember me? I am the one you gave the dollar to." He then stuck out his hand to shake and he gave me the dollar back. I smiled and then I said to him, "Have a great day, I know I just did, keep it and just keep passing it on." When you pass it on, it often comes back to you. When you take advantage of a time to help someone, to do the right thing, to seize an opportunity to pass it on, it will come back to you, one way or another.

As is the case several times during the completion of this book, something happened causing me to add to or finish one of the stories I had written. Such is this case with the young man that borrowed the dollar at UHD that day. As you will read about in the final chapter, I graduated on May 18, 2013 finally with my long sought after college degree. It was a wonderful day and I do not want to steal my own thunder by giving away anything but what I will say is this. I delivered the keynote commencement speech that day in front of 18,000 people at Minute Maid Park, including my children. After the event was finally over and everyone poured out in the streets surrounding Minute Maid Park, it was a challenge to locate my family. As you might imagine, there was a sea of caps and gowns surrounded by proud, loving friends and family, all taking pictures, sweating in the hot sun at 2 pm on a Sunday. One of my children said on the cell phone that they were waiting at home plate. I stopped for just a moment to get my bearings. The moment I stopped, peering into the stadium to determine where I was, a young man holding a rose boldly spoke to me. He said, "Hey, your speech was great, do you remember me? Startled, staring into the hot sun, I acted as if I might but I really did not. He said, "I am the person that borrowed the dollar from you that day at UHD and then I gave it back. Remember? You said pass it on, so I did." I looked at him, realizing that it was indeed the same young man, I said, "You have to be kidding me!" I said, "You are in my book." He smiled, we shook hands and I said, "Do you have a name?" "Eric," he said, "Eric Ross." I said, "Well Eric Ross, do you mind if I use your name in my book?" He said, "Go ahead, that's great." We exchanged a few more pleasantries and then parted ways. As I walked around to that home plate area to find my children, I could only think that the chances of our running into each other were zero. Another testimonial to the master plan I have talked about throughout the book. What it caused me to do that very night was to go back and finish my thoughts in this section. I wanted to conclude by saying is that they do have a name. They all have names and they all have needs. His name is Eric Ross and he inspires me to the core of my being.

Find your Major Opportunity to <u>pass it on</u>!

No matter what age you are when you finally get it, when you realize there are "Major Opportunities," to pass it on that go beyond just extending a simple courtesy or a small measure of kindness. By "getting it," I refer to that moment in your life when you finally decide to apply your own God given talents not just as a vehicle to achieve individual success, but when you decide to shift those skills and abilities to benefit something special, something bigger than you and I. For me, that major opportunity opened because of ex-my brother in law, Craig Schuster. He is and always will be the salt of the earth, they do not make them any better than him. Having said that, often it takes another person to open a door of opportunity, to help you see it staring you square in the face. Craig opened a very big door for me, one that would change my life. Craig Schuster was on the board of director's for a children's home near San Antonio, built the year I was born in 1957. It was originally Medina Children's Home and is now under the umbrella of The Arms of Hope. The home is located in the rolling hills near Bandera, Texas and is home to about 135 kids from all ages and all walks of life that are in need.

According to their site, "Arms of Hope is a 501(c) (3) not-for-profit Christian care organization that assists children and single-mother families in need. Arms of Hope's facilities include Medina Children's Home (60 miles northwest of San Antonio) and Boles Children's Home (40 miles northeast of Dallas). The facilities have over 135 years combined experience in comprehensive residential care programs for children. Arms of Hope also reach disadvantaged children in their own neighborhoods in various communities with its Outreach Ministry programs. Through its Residential Child Care, Together, College and Career, Right Start, and Outreach Ministry programs, Arms of Hope is committed to providing a safe haven and Christian environment for children and single-mother families by helping them avoid homelessness, poverty, abuse and neglect and by leading them to lives of sustaining and productive citizenship. Our residents attend public school, nearby universities or trade schools and participate in school, church and campus activities. The Arms of Hope does not receive any federal or state grants. Instead, Arms of Hope relies on caring individuals, businesses, civic groups, churches and foundations for funding and volunteer support.

Craig has been involved doing work for the home for many years. When he was an architect for the Pappas Family restaurants, he had leaned on them every year as a source of support, for many years. There is a dinner held traditionally at The River Oaks Country Club and typically, each year, without the benefit of serving any alcoholic beverages, the dinner will rake in about $65,000 to $75,000 in one evening. For years, one of Craig's friends, Greg Hurst, Channel 11 news anchor served as our emcee for the dinner, he is a great man.

One year back in 2003, I received a call from Craig. He simply said, "David how would you and your wife like to have free tickets to a really good dinner to help some under-privileged children?" He said, "Normally, they sell for $125 a piece but this year, they are free for you, you can be our guest." I liked the sound of free, so I accepted quickly. The dinner was a wonderful experience. Four hundred people attended the event that year with a nice meal served but the evening belonged to Medina's children (Arm of Hope). The dinner was all about them, serving the needs of the home as it was obvious that any funds raised at the dinner would go a long way towards helping kids in need. Several of the kids came down from the home with house parents, and a few would even muster the courage to speak at the dinner.

"Major Opportunities"

It was a wonderfully inspiring evening and we raised $75,000 that night on behalf of the kids of Medina.

Year 2, 2004, Craig called again. I took the call and this time he said, "David how would you and your wife like to BUY tickets to a really good dinner?" "The tickets are only $125, but for you they are $125." Remembering the free dinner the year before, remembering the great experience we had, knowing that it was not a high price to pay to help kids, I said yes. He also said before I got off the phone, "I really want you to be on the steering committee this year too." I agreed quickly, not really knowing what they meant, but trusting that what Craig does, one should do also. My assignment was to plan the menu that year, negotiating with River Oaks to get the best deal I could. That year we had 467 and, we had Crème Brule, and yes, Crème Brule is one of my favorites. Craig let me add a silent auction for the first time and we hit about $5,000 in that effort. That year we hit $78,000.

My boss Ernie bought a table in the name of Palais Royal and my typically somber, analytical boss who refuses to admit he had emotions, was clearly touched to the core as was his wonderful wife Annabel. I know because there were no dry eyes that night when one of the young ladies raised at the home, "Jane", got up to the podium to talk about her life now at Texas A&M with dreams of becoming an attorney. She courageously stood up and told this crowd of 467 that her mom never really wanted her. Fighting back tears she said, "Medina wanted me." She described the "Major Opportunities" she had been afforded and how her life had changed because of Medina's love and outreach. It was a touching evening all the way around, there was not a dry eye in the house, including my own.

Year 3, 2005, my administrative assistant said, "Craig is on the phone again, Mr. Slaughter." "No kidding," I said. Thinking I was going to have the opportunity to buy a table this time, instead he asked me to split a table with him and then asked me to serve as chairman that year which meant wearing many hats of responsibility but Craig was up to the challenge of mentoring me. Major Opportunity was now knocking and I had to open the door.

Craig had confidence in me it appeared, after all, I was running a billion dollar company and if I could keep fourteen districts managers in toe, surely I could handle 500 or 600 hundred people. I made some significant changes that year that Craig never even blinked once with hesitation. First, I increased the number of items in the silent auction. Second, we refined the bidding process to bring in a more reasonable amount of money based upon the quality of each item. Third, I started to add many more driven, committed people to the steering committee in an effort to build bench strength for the future of the dinner.

That year, I decided the move the location of the dinner to the Westin Galleria, as I wanted 600 people. I extended the silent auction and added a live auction with three key items. The items included my wife's Amegy Suite for the Astros, a big TV and a custom fish tank from the Fish Gallery, the same company that had installed one in my study a few years prior. It was the only year I was able to secure him for an auction, but this first year I landed the Houston Rodeo auctioneer, Bill Booher. He only did it one year but, boy oh boy, was it worth it. Adding a live auction on top of a silent auction was a logistical nightmare as you might imagine but I had added a bench to our steering committee that was unmatched.

When it came time for the auction, not exactly knowing what might happen as I had rolled the dice with Craig's complete support and the first item up for bid was the Amegy Suite. The Astros were hot but its value at retail was probably $2500 max, I thought. When it hit $10,500, instead of saying, "10,600?" this Houston rodeo auctioneer did the best thing he could have possibly done, he turned to my wife's boss, an Executive VP of Amegy—sitting next to Mayor Bill White and with the voice of an angel he said to her, "Could we have another suite?" She said yes immediately, received a rousing round of applause from the crowd and in an instant we had two big sales, one for $10,500 and one for $10,600. Next was the fish tank and it went for $6,000 and the final item, the TV probably worth $1800 was up to $7400 and when he said sold for $7400, the old man stood up and said to

"Major Opportunities"

him, "Give it the guy that said $7300, I will write you a check and he can have the TV." So in a matter of minutes we had hit over $40,000 with a live auction we added. The silent auction raised $12,000 that year, someone put a $25,000 check in the plate and in one evening, we took the dinner from its traditional $75,000 to $143,000.

That year, I met two twins we will refer to as "Jill" and "Janie." That would turn out to become a life-changing door that would open, close and now reopen as I write this book. For three years "Jill" and "Janie," age 9, then 10, then 11 who live at the children's home came down to be a part of the dinner. Two of those three years, they went home with my family to spend the night. We would take them to church with us the next morning and then they would ride back with the other kids or with one of the house parents returning to the home that afternoon. It was a positive experience for our own kids to spend time with them, their manners were wonderful and they enjoyed playing with our daughters. Interestingly, after the dinner each year the first thing the two of them wanted to do was to get me to take them by McDonalds, it was a tradition we started and held onto. My job each of those two years was to lag behind after the rest of our large family had gotten ready and I was to micromanage getting the girls to finish getting ready and then bring them on to church.

The first year we kept them overnight, also my first year as Chairman, I called upstairs to encourage them that it was time to leave but I heard no answer. I went to the bottom of the stairs and called out again to them, but still no answer. I went upstairs and said, "Girls c'mon, we have to go." I walked in one of my daughter's room; they were both on the floor crying. Ignorantly, I said to them "What's up, what's going on girls." Jill turned to me and said, "Janie has lost the chain to her locket, it's in the carpet, and we can't find it, we have to find it." "What locket, what are **you** two talking about?" She showed me the locket and as she opened it, it held a tiny picture of their mother, missing her two front teeth, the same mother that I knew lived four blocks away in a tear me down house in Bellaire, the same mother I knew did not want them anymore. I swallowed hard and thought to myself how incredible was this love, this unconditional love that these two precious little angels still had for their one and only mother despite her denial of them as hers. I thought to myself, this is why we do what we do. That is why I did it as Chairman two more years. I told Craig, "I will be chairman till I tell you I am not," with him not knowing the rest of the story until now. I served two more terms as chairman, in large part due to my understanding of why we do it, because we should, because we can, because there are "Major Opportunities" to pass it on. Jill and Janie are typical of the kind of wonderful children that the "Arms of Hope," provides for.

The next year, 2006 was a record year in net proceeds for the Medina Children's Home. (Arms of Hope) dinner. Barbara Bush rejected an invitation to speak but she sent a friend of hers and his name was Kenneth Starr. He served as the special prosecutor against Bill Clinton in the Monica Lewinski scandal. What I did not know until that evening is that he is one of the finest, most polite, Christian men I have ever met. What I did not know was that Kenneth Starr was twenty-six and one in front of the Supreme Court. What I also did not know was that he would speak two more times at our dinners for no charge over the next few years. That year we had 656 people attend the event and I turned the silent auction loose on the lions I had been feeding, a.k.a. — the steering committee, and it was a homerun, raising $92,000 this time on the silent auction alone. The live auction had Lance Armstrong's Tour De France Jersey #7 (sorry Lance), Roger Clemon's crystal ball from the World Series and a few other key items; all totaled we hit $263,000 that year. We accomplished all of that due to loving charitable people who opened their hearts first and then their pocketbooks wide, all for a good cause, the children.

My final year as Chairman, 2007, we kept on hitting home runs for the kids all year long. The infrastructure was now firmly in place, and the dinner would continue hitting the intended mark. My own company, Stage Stores Inc., sent twenty-one people to the dinner occupying three tables, representing Palais Royal here

"Major Opportunities"

in Houston. We hit another $250,000 with over 550 in attendance at the dinner. We had built something from inside that would continue to last for a long time.

I say all of this to offer inspiration as to what can happen when you open the doors that are there wide open. I tell you this lengthy story not so you can give the credit to any one individual as it was the work of so many. I do suggest that one person like Craig Schuster who plants seeds that can grow, can have an influence on so many as the seeds grow into trees. Craig opened that first door of opportunity and it was up to me to keep on opening more doors. Every-time I knocked, another door would open. You too can apply the talent you have in business to help worthy causes in your own community. Those are your doors of major opportunity, so go find one now!

It is not just about giving your money; it is about sharing your passion, your energy and your time to serve others. I will soon begin the pursuit of my Master's in Non-profit Management at the university I love, the University of Houston-Downtown, knowing full well that I have already seen and experienced a master plan once that will make the path easier to walk. I tell you that when we see an open door with children standing inside we must rush in as the doors of major opportunity fly wide open.

So go find the right Major Opportunity for you!

~ Chapter 13 ~
"Major Opportunity Success Stories"

"The Norris Family"
Photo Compliments of Mom and Dad

As we move into the final chapter of "Major Opportunities," I determined it was important to share some examples I uncovered in which people walked through some unique doors of success. As I reflected upon the stories I collected, I set aside my journal notes and did some research of my own pertaining to successes attained throughout history, across diverse fields, representing doors that were often forced open. I discovered that in many cases there had been a higher rate of failure than of success in the examples

I studied. I concluded that many more doors had closed than had opened and in many cases, doors have to be broken down or knocked down in order to locate and maximized the "Major Opportunities." I also discovered that many of the examples belonged to some of the most successful people in history — names that most would recognize not for failure, but for the greatness of their successes recognized over the years. Time, history, and perspective do have a way of differentiating the pride, hard work and personal dedication of one's work from the short term perceived value of that work to mankind.

A history of "Major Opportunities"

As I looked back in time, I accumulated a list of people who failed repeatedly until they met with success or those who did not receive credit for their success until long after they were gone. As a reminder, anyone of us can walk through opportunity doors to accomplish what we set as a goal. History has a wonderful way of allowing future generations to share in the achievements of others. Some examples I discovered included; Henry Ford, Socrates, Albert Einstein, Thomas Edison, Orville and Wilbur Wright, Emily Dickinson, Stephen King, Walt Disney, JK Rowling, Vincent van Gogh, Sidney Poitier, Oprah Winfrey, Wolfgang Amadeus Mozart, Ludwig van Beethoven, Michael Jordon, Elvis Presley, Abraham Lincoln, Colonel Sanders, and Charlie Chaplin. This is only a short list that represents the large number of people that once failed miserably only to turn out to be some of the people we all remember best.

After devoting much of this book to doors of opportunity waiting to open, I would be remiss if I did not share some of the major success stories of yours I found along the way. Over this past year, I met many special people whose personal stories they shared were inspiring to me in so many ways. Each story I include offers an example of a door someone walked through, despite challenges, adversity and pain. The stories are real, the people are real, and the examples of success demonstrate the power of what one person has to offer as they endeavor to do their best in life. No one was required to reveal their story, often they appeared during an open-ended discussion or in the course of a friendly conversation. In the end, these stories, these special people, these unique opportunities caused me to decide to continue my search for your stories offering testimony of the opportunities hidden behind the doors of opportunity. It became the driving force to begin my next book project, "Major Opportunities of the Heart, the Soul and the Mind."

The Norris Family, "Sometimes doors open wide for Pairs"

The first story I watched unfold with great inspiration, love and respect from afar for a grandmother, a husband and a wife and two precious new souls born into this world of major opportunity. It is a story of the beauty of life that sometimes, arrives, in pairs. It is the story of Carter and Brody Norris and is sure to become a story of "Major Opportunities", to be and recorded over years of watching doors open over and over again for both of them." This story begins with two expectant parents, Elissa and Josh Norris. Many of us know of the excitement, the curiosity, even the agony and the stress of bringing children into this world. Brody and Carter were born July 7, 2012 at Women's Hospital in Houston weighing 3.4 pounds and 3.1 pounds respectively. They were born at thirty-four weeks after their mother, Elissa, (mama) had been hospitalized for three months, flat on her back and then the boys remained in the hospital for weeks after mom went home.

"Major Opportunities"

Brody and Carter Norris
Photo Compliments of "Mom and Dad"

Jumping forward seven months, they are caught up now to normal weight, as they weigh between fifteen and sixteen pounds respectively. I met with the boy's grandmother Patty, Gigi they call her, to interview her, and I asked her to recount what stood out the most about these two precious boys and these loving parents. "Josh probably would blush to know that I am writing this but I was told by Elissa's mom that one of the things she remembers most looking back was that every single night after he worked all day, Josh would be at the hospital. Any one of you who have had a loved one in the hospital for an extended period understands that between the working, the parking, the parking fees, the food and the driving, well let's say, it has to be called an "act of love." I asked Patty what she remembers about Elissa pertaining during that long three-month stay. She spoke with resolve in her voice of her daughter's patience, of her commitment to putting the boys first and of her strong faith.

When I talked with supermom, Elissa, she told me that one might think that when she had to go home leaving those two precious twins in the hospital that you might think it would be impossible. Instead, she told me that once again it was her faith in knowing that she needed to go home, get some rest, and prepare herself for the journey ahead. It motivated her to get better herself so that she could be strong for her boys. I continue to see the beautiful pictures that keep showing up on Facebook of the twins and they get cuter and cuter and cuter each day. They just recently celebrated one year and the door of opportunity has opened for them to begin to become toddlers. I am truly inspired by these wonderful, loving, unselfish, parents and by the love of grandparents. This door is wide open as the world watches as Brody and Carter Norris learn to crawl, to walk, to run and to knock on their doors of "Major Opportunities."

Randy Krinsky, "No butter crème cake required"

I met this next person my first semester in Dr. Gulati's microbiology class. Remember, it was my only B, but a B I am very proud of, because I earned it. Randy Krinsky was just like me in only one respect that I am aware of, he was in that class with me. Other than that, we are completely different. We are different in the respect that he made an A and I made a B. We are different in the sense that he excels in math and science and I struggle. We are different in the respect that Randy will never need a butter crème cake in order to throw himself on the mercy of an excellent UHD professor. Finally, we are different in the respect that he received the honor fall 2012 as a recipient of the Hispanic Genealogical Society scholarship. One more fact I discovered during my research is that his seventh great grandfather was the co-founder of San Antonio, Texas. Randy, a senior, is a history major and I do not think he broke a sweat during any of our tests, our labs or during any of the high-level microbiology discussions. Having said that, we are the same I believe in one more respect, in that we both tried as hard as we could, we both are inspired to do the very best we can do, we were both rewarded for our efforts and we both graduated on May 18, 2013 at Minute Maid Park in Houston, Texas.

"Major Opportunities"

Myrtie Groves, "Attitude is Everything"

The next story, written as I first walked through the doors at UHD the first week is about a remarkable employee at UHD. Much to my dismay, I was required that first semester back in school to pass a test to verify if I could by-pass a required math class by the State of Texas. I was required to go directly to the University Testing Center, door 201. Sadly, some things do not change in thirty years, you still have to pass math in order to earn a college diploma. During the painful process of attempting this feat, I met and be befriended a wonderful UHD employee Myrtie Groves, a Testing Specialist #1 in the center.

Myrtie's smile, her positive attitude, and her compassion for what a return aging student was going through in order to reach a goal, was comforting and reassuring to me. She set me at ease from the minute I met her. Attitude is everything and Myrtie's attitude is very special. Perhaps I should have taken her advice and should have studied for the CLEP test. The results suggested that I needed help with math and this guy, who was responsible for half a billion dollars in annual sales just a few years prior, was required to enroll in two math classes in order to graduate. I now had to face my fear. Myrtie's smile is contagious and she can always turn a bad day into a better one. She set my fears at ease immediately. I still stop and visit her from time to time just because I always feel better after I see and talk to her. She is one UHD employee that reflects what excellence is about.

Chris Cordoza, "A family Affair"

I met Chris Cardoza in a "Math for Liberal Arts," class. Chris acted as if he was part of our study group as a method to improve his math skills. The fact of the matter is Chris coached us all more than he was by any of us during weeks of study as a group. I knew I had to hear Chris's story, it appealed to me that he was working full time, a father, a husband, all while taking a full time load of classes. His G.P.A. was the same as mine that semester, a 4.0, but his final math average was 109. That, which seemed unfair, but completely understandable to me now, — I hold no grudges Chris.

His story though is not about math, it is about family, commitment, and vision. In the midst of our first discussion, they shared a personal story with me that was very powerful. It is a story that exemplifies how unexpected doors of opportunity in life may open. This door happens to be one that parents do not wish they had to go through, one not recognized as a door of opportunity by any parent. Chris and Michelle explained that when their daughter Taylor was thirteen, a door opened that they did not see opening for them.

They told me about bringing dinner for families to at the Ronald McDonald House here in Houston. They prepared four pans of lasagna and went by to drop the food off after working all day. Then told me that exactly one week later, with their daughter complaining of headaches, they would learn that their own thirteen-year-old daughter Taylor, had a golf ball-size tumor on her brain. Therefore, one week after taking food to families facing crisis, they themselves would be back at the Ronald McDonald House, facing a personal family crisis of their own.

Taylor says NO!

I swallowed the large lump in my throat, as I stated softly that things always seem to happen for a reason, and then they continued with the story. Despite the fact that doctors had a rather challenging prognosis for Taylor's long-term future, as a family, as a husband and wife, they played the cards they were dealt. Not completely understanding the difficulty that she would face in fighting this physical challenge, their daughter would never accept that that this set-back was fatal, debilitating or even that it would serve as any tangible interference to what she had in mind, she had other plans. As they proudly explained, she is now on the dean's list at the University of Houston main campus and she is

"Major Opportunities"

committed to working in child development as her career goal, Taylor plans to help other children.

Instead of accepting defeat based upon a doctor's prediction that her IQ might not be good, Taylor chose through hard work, persistence and through character to make them eat their words. The doors are wide open for one bright soul who took on her sickness, proving many great Houston doctors to be so wrong. Her opportunities are ahead of her, I cannot wait to see the doors that open for her. "Major Opportunities," occur during pain, suffering or adversity and Taylor saw these as temporary set-backs, not as obstacles.

Chris passionately relayed to me that his life inspiration is his wife. She too went back to school to complete her degree during this ordeal as he said, "If she could do it, I knew I could. My wife is my cheerleader. For sixteen years she has believed in me, she is my best friend." He described her as, "Wonderful, intelligent, and strong and she always has my back."

Major opportunity successes are not just individual successes or accomplishments. They can be a result of the life decisions we make. Another wonderful individual, just like Michelle, is capable of pointing or leading the way to a door, leading the way, by her example. Sometimes, they show one the door, sometimes they open the door, sometimes they push you through the door, only to be waiting on the other side to pat you on the back, joining with you in the "Major Opportunities," of success. People like Chris and Michelle are willing to look for and go through the next door with you as Chris did with me in our "Math for Liberal Arts Majors."

Chris explained that one of the things he and his daughter received last Christmas from Michelle was two framed diplomas, one for each of them. Even though Chris and Taylor are both still working towards a diploma, she presented them each with their own framed diploma, displaying them prominently on the wall in the study next to the one she received in 2010. She told him, "This is what it will look like; this is where it will go." Chris told me later that he felt a chill go up his spine as he stared at his own vision of what was ahead. Going through a door of opportunity occurs due to an ability to envision a result and then moving directly toward it and is often the result of the inspiration of another.

Chris, Michelle and Taylor have walked through the door of higher education together, at different ages, at different times, and for different reasons. Their stories address the meaning of vision, purpose and opportunity. Their story reflects moving courageously to reach a goal seen in front of them and they are inspiring to me. Chris wrapped up this open door of opportunity when he said, "I am going to go wherever this door leads me next, but my wife opened this door by showing me it can be done and now it will be done." What he must know, is that he, his wife, and his daughter and his story will inspire others, like you, to know that those doors are out there for you as well!

James Blake, "The Tallest Man in the Room"

The next story is one that was always there, ever since I went back to school two years ago. It was right in front of me and I just had never opened the door. I had seen it every week for almost two years. Finally, I knocked and the door opened wide and the man that opened the door is James. James has been attending the university for as long as I have, perhaps longer. We have had several classes together. We have talked from time to time but only from a distance, only through a door that was slightly ajar. What I learned from James so far is too much for one chapter to contain. I had made an appointment with him recently in an effort to finish getting his story after class. Instead, one of our assignments was to prepare and to read a ceremonial speech in front of each other. In class that day, I heard his story prematurely as he read it to all of us. His story is one of inspiration. He recounted the ordeal of going through, surviving and adjusting to a major stroke. With great strength and resolution in his voice, he shared with us the challenges that were real for him but most importantly, he focused upon the opportunities he sees in front of him each day, the

"Major Opportunities"

same ones he said are our own "Major Opportunities.," as well. Selfishly, I was writing as he spoke but what was striking to me were the looks on the faces of his classmates. They were listening, and thinking and, it was no longer a ceremonial speech, it was real and we were his captive audience

James, a man in a wheel chair, was the man standing the tallest in class this that day. He said he never stopped trying, nor should we. He did not present a false, rosy picture of everything in his life; he shared the reality of pain, as he offered hope and encouragement. He offered the same advice that he gives his family as a loving spouse and father, "Use your brain, use your body and never stop trying." I confirmed that often success is affected by what a person recognizes as their potential to succeed and it is directly impacted by what they choose to do about it. I verified it has more to do with maintaining a positive, caring, attitude than it does with having possessions, fame or fortune.

Interestingly, part of the group exercise was to provide feedback after his speech. I am not quite sure why it came out of my mouth but one of my comments was that the speech was too long. Quickly realizing I was an idiot for suggesting that, before I could recover, thankfully, someone else jumped in. The same professor of ours who professionally shoots straight from the hip with us because after thirty years he still cares deeply, one who openly demonstrates a burning desire to coach, train and mentor well beyond what teaching defines or requires, stepped in and said, "Well, no it wasn't too long," and he was right.

James' door is wide open for those who want to enter it and I am the one who has gained by walking through that door. We will no longer just pass in the hall, we will look each other in the eyes with a deeper meaning and we will both know by one look that we share, that we mean it and, that we care. It is people like James that make me want to do better, to be better, and that make me want to show a little more kindness than I did the day before. Heaven can wait, for people like James Blake.

John Locke, Opportunity is what YOU make of it!

The next major opportunity success story provides is an example of what one will find when they open a brand new door. I met John Locke during a roundtable meeting with the Student Government Association to discuss student dorms. As John introduced himself, a familiar story emerged as he spoke of enrolling in UHD with a plan to transfer in the next semester or two to the main campus. Instead, he explained that he had also developed a deep love for the university, one that rang familiar to my ears. He said it would be near impossible now to drag him away. I asked him to share his story with me in detail.

We met the next morning for breakfast and I quickly realized that this is another one of those revolving doors where we could help each other in some way or another. Doors that open do not always open because of a knock, sometimes you just walk into one that seems important or interesting. John openly and honestly shared having a rough start in life. He told me of dropping out of high school, only to obtain a GED later than he should have. He did not go into specific details, he was just very forthright about playing around all the while, and he did not know that it was a story with which I could relate. He shared a vision of community involvement that was overpowering and expressed a commitment of wanting to give back to the community as one of his top priorities in life. John defined as the reason he chose UHD and subsequently fell in love with the school with one word, "Pride." As I left breakfast, I reflected to myself that each person has something unique waiting behind a door of opportunity, something worth looking for. You just have to open the door sometimes by saying, "Hello, I would like to get to know you and walk right on in."

I took my research to another level, asking him if I could interview his mom. I stated, "My guess is there is a story of success behind your story of success John," He graciously provided her number and as a professional courtesy, he called her in advance to let her know I wanted to visit. A few days later, I called Cheryl, and as we chatted, I validated that I was right. Behind a recovery from pain and defeat, behind a story of going the wrong way, is a patient loving mother who kept on believing and hoping but with tough love, she had to stop enabling. She spoke of her deep love and respect for John. She was brutally honest as she mentioned the wrong path he had chosen for a while but she said now she sees the light he is projecting all around him. She is glad he is actively involved at school and is proud he is connecting with the right peers at UHD as a leader. She was pleased to hear positive feedback that he has "Major Opportunities," ahead of him.

A final message from John's story is one that I thought diligently about before including it in this chapter because it is very personal and private. I did not bring it up in my conversation with his mother, and I chose to go back and re-visit the opportunity in my heart. John had mentioned that his mom had become pregnant at the young age of fifteen with him those twenty-eight years ago and faced with being a young single mom with no support in place, she faced a decision as to what to do. She chose to have the baby and we got John Locke. She has worked as a manager at McDonalds now for twenty-eight years. I am not here to suggest that a woman's right to choose is right or wrong, because surely it is their choice. What I will say is that Cheryl chose the right door because I know John and John's "Major Opportunities," are ahead of him due to a tough personal decision a great mother made. I suspect it was just as tough for her to have tough love that she applied when John had went astray as it might have been to struggle with the decision she made to have him. One person, one tough decision and one mother who keeps on believing in you, makes all the difference in the world.

Ivan Sanchez, "A Mother's lead, A Leader learns to Lead"

Another success story I want you to read about is one of love, compassion, energy and enthusiasm. I met Ivan Sanchez when I shared a public deliberation class with him and he was

David Slaughter

the President of the SGA. On occasion, he is accused of being too strong willed—of not just leading others to water but insisting that they drink it too. Honestly, I find him refreshing. I did not understand where his passion and zest for life came from until I spotted a picture on his wall and eventually pressured him to give me the story behind it and it became the story.

I see a lot of Ivan in myself. He is an energetic, big vision, never-say-no kind of a man, a leader who is obsessed about getting to the top. He is a young man to whom people say, "Slow down, you will burn out," when they just cannot keep up or when they prefer being mediocre. The story I obtained came in one interview with him. During that interview, I validated where his love, passion and commitment come from, they come from deep inside his heart. He has a picture framed in his office of a beautiful woman that I was to learn, was his mother.

As we visited, he talked mostly of his mother and of his family during the early years that they lived in Columbia. "She was a lead prosecutor," he said, "verbal physical threats against their lives in Columbia were typical in her profession," he said. "She shielded us as the best she good," he said. He continued the story, "Once, someone sent word to my mother that the next time her kids got on the bus would be the last time they did so. So, she bundled us up and without a job, or an income, and barely speaking English, she brought us to the land of major opportunity—to America." He told me that she learned English and focused on her education and that eventually she founded her own business that has since become a multi-million dollar mortgage company in Houston, Texas. This all came about because of one woman's vision of success, her hard work and a determination to protect her young ones at her top priority.

Sadly, he then explained that at the age of forty-nine his mother passed away, on his dad's birthday. Fighting back emotion by speaking more deliberately and slowly, he explained that she instilled in him a burning desire to apply every ounce of his heart and soul to whatever he does. He said he misses her terribly, as one might expect. Now I truly understand why her picture is what he stares into from across his desk during long days and nights that he spends in the office. The tone of his voice was one of sincerity, of appreciation and of admiration for what she accomplished in the forty-nine years she was alive with full appreciation of the sacrifices she had made along the way. Ivan's story is not unlike many I have heard this year and it reinforces what I have repeated throughout this book; that the influence of one person, of one mentor, of one single person who consistently demonstrates they care, can be one of the most powerful forces driving successful people. Derived from a love for life, a love for doing your best, and a love for helping others, that distinguishes great leaders from others.

A'Tondra Gilstrap, "A Mother, a Leader, a Doctor"

The final story I will share is one about one of the Major Opportunity students I met at the President's Community Breakfast. Her name is A'Tondra Gilstrap. This amazing mother of four has managed to accomplish what most could not fathom. Setting her sights on becoming a doctor was no easy task after spending years working in the private sector. When I heard her speak at the breakfast, I knew I had to write her story. I marched right up to her and told her that she was incredible and that I wanted her story and then I chased her I pestered her incessantly until the story was recorded. To me, she defines what excellence is all about.

Our meeting began with me getting to meet three of her four children and introducing them to one of mine as well. We took care of their needs, got them situated and then visited for about forty-five minutes. I confirmed this day that she is a deep, passionate, articulate thinker that places being a mother at the top of her priorities. She was born in Tulsa, Oklahoma and at the age of six months, moved to Lagos, Nigeria. She then at the age of nine and a half moved to Houston, Texas. I listened as she shared her sense of failure over not obtaining her degree when she was at

Baylor University in Waco, Texas years prior. I could appreciate when she explained she had to go to work to survive as a young mother. She made it clear that her path in life had not been an easy one and her support group had been small. Gaining more respect for her with every passing minute, I listened as she explained having the desire to reach her dream at thirty to become a doctor of physical medicine and rehabilitation. She has a 3.21 GPA in the scholar's academy at UHD and will graduate in spring 2014.

I asked her if there had been someone who influenced her, more than another did this time back. As tears welled up in her eyes, she hesitated and wiping the tears away as she said, "I always start crying when someone asks me that question." She said, "About three semesters ago I went into my professor's office, Dr. Jerry Johnson, and I looked him square in the eyes and said, "Dude, I am done, I am dropping out, I just can't do this." She described him as brilliant as she reflected upon his response. He said he would have none of that kind of talk. With some indignation at the thought that she was considering leaving, he said, "If you do that, I will find you and bring you back, because you are brilliant, you are special, you are super woman." He continued, "You are a high caliber, capable woman." They talked more and she left and changed her mind. He changed her life. She said she left with a greater sense of pride in herself because she knew she just needed someone that she admired, someone who had demonstrated through their actions they care, to tell her to keep on going. She needed someone that she respected as much as she does Dr. Jerry Johnson, to confirm that she could win this time.

The Influence of One Who Cared to Say No

After hearing of the influence Dr. Johnson had upon her, I simply had to track him down. I needed to tell him face-to-face how significant his role had been in her life. He is a very busy man, A'Tondra had warned me as much but after several trips to the sixth floor, I finally cornered him and I found his door to be wide open. He comes across exactly as A'Tondra described him, as a humble, caring, deliberate man. I asked him to comment about his recollection of that day she described to me, a day where he said outright to her, "Oh no you don't!"

He agreed to provide some comments for me to include in my book. He wrote the following, "In many ways, A'Tondra is an archetypal UHD student, but in other ways, she is an outlier. She comes to UHD with a cadre of hurdles and it is those hurdles that allow her victories to be monumental. She came to UHD with a mixture of determined humility, and a commanding conviction that she is on the right path to improving her future, and that of her family. Many UHD students are similar. When I first met A'Tondra, she struck me as fiercely intelligent, one wanting to rise to the challenges we set before her. However, she was also waiting; waiting for someone to tell her that it was OK for her to be excellent; it was OK to be successful. She needed validation, encouragement and a sense of personal accountability. The UHD faculty was happy to oblige. Once the UHD faculty provided these 'licenses' for success, there was nothing to stop her in pursuing her dreams. Since then, she has tackled her studies with a vengeance that all faculty love to see in their students."

To me, A'Tondra is Superwoman. I think back about to the challenges that I faced as an undergraduate student, to how much support I had to help me be successful, and I am humbled by what she has been able to accomplish. I realize how easy I had it. She is raising a family, and doing it phenomenally. I have had the chance to meet her children, and I can only hope that my children are as intelligent and well behaved as hers are at a similar age. In addition to raising her children well, and being successful in her studies, she also somehow manages to put a roof over her family's heads, provide food and a strong moral compass for them, and still she shows up every day with a smile on her face and a sense of gratitude for those trying to help her.

Dr. Johnson said, "I was humbled by A'Tondra's acknowledgement of my efforts on her behalf. However, I am no different from the majority of the faculty at UHD. Scholarship and research are the metrics by which faculty are judged by their peers, and is the primary mechanisms by which we can elevate the name of UHD in the national and international view. In coming to UHD, a teaching institution, the faculty made a choice to focus on the success of our students. It is our primary responsibility, and our scholarship is secondary. We spend more time with our students, both in and out of the classroom, than faculty at research-intensive universities. In doing so, we have less time to pursue the level of scholarship that faculty at nearby research institutes are able to dedicate. Thus, the UHD faculty makes sacrifices on the behalf of our students, because we love to be in the classroom, helping them achieve their dreams. A'Tondra is the type of student that makes this an easy choice, and a worthy sacrifice. While faculty at most other institutions measure the height of their success by how many books or papers they publish, the faculty at UHD has a different measure. UHD faculty will never stand as tall as when our students are standing on our shoulders reaching for their dreams."

As I have said repeatedly to you, the power of one person, the influence of one caring, giving individual makes all the difference in the world. Professors like Dr. Jerry Johnson are the ones who give generously of their time, of their knowledge and in the case of A'Tondra; they become the mentor of a lifetime. UHD is lucky to have him and he is one of many humble ones who make UHD a place one can find their "Major Opportunities."

Not only does A'Tondra have a great GPA, recently her research was published for the first time. The article is entitled, "Global and Local Methods of Accessing Nociception Drosophilarva." The link to find it is http:www.jove.com/video/3837/local-global-methods-assessinh-thermal-nociception-drosophila. It is a remarkable achievement that an undergraduate student gets consideration for published material. It distinguishes her very early on in her quest to become a doctor and it sets the bar high bar high for the great things she will accomplish going forward.

"Major Opportunities"

At the risk of drawing more tears, I asked her what she wanted for her children in life and she said she wants them to find three things, "Confidence, balance and success." We concluded our interview, as we both had other commitments, and as we parted, I left with a strong sense of what it feels like to capture a story that defines, "Major Opportunities of Success." A'Tondra Gilstrap is continuing her incredible journey through those opportunity doors we know well. The final message she wanted to share is one that resonates with me today. She said, "I learned about life the hard way, all by myself, which was tough, but regardless of how tough it is, people need to dream." and she added, "Everyone does need to know though that people do need help from others."

I know there will continue to be many more inspiring stories to document and to share with you. No matter what, I will not stop recording your stories in my journals. Because of you and your inspiring stories, I am committed to share those next examples of "Major Opportunities," in my next book. Like each of you, I too will continue knocking on, opening and walking through doors of human experience called doors of opportunity in an effort to enjoy the excitement of life.

This book is not about one great university experience and it is not just about one person or even about one story of success. It is about being who YOU can be by being all YOU can be. It is about being brave and courageous in your personal search for the revolving doors of "Major Opportunities." It is about sharing YOUR passion, about finding a healthy balance, about giving back, and it is about including as many others in your vision as you can. It is about understanding that without them, the journey to the top becomes wary and difficult. When opening the doors we have discussed it is much more fun and much more satisfying to have others do it with you, to have others go with you on your way to the top. This story is about accepting that life has its obstacles, its hills and valleys, but in the end, one must be ready and willing to explore doors with the anticipation of finding something new and exciting behind each one of them.

David Slaughter

MR. DAVID SLAUGHTER
STUDENT REPRESENTATIVE

Photos Compliments of the University of Houston-Downtown

I close this book on Sunday evening, May 18, 2013, by describing another great day, similar to how I did at the beginning of this book. This truly was another great day. It was the kind of a day on which super bowls should be played. Today, I finally walked across the stage at Minute Maid Park with 1,043 of my fellow students, to accept my college diploma. Today, I received my bachelor's degree with a B.S. in Interdisciplinary Studies with and a Minor in Communication from the University of Houston-Downtown, notably, with a 3.92 GPA.

Photo Compliments of the University of Houston-Downtown

"Major Opportunities"

The ceremony, attended by four of my five precious children, ranging in ages from twenty-eight to ten, close family members, friends and 18,000 people in the audience, all of them honoring the 2013 graduating class of the University of Houston-Downtown UHD. I worked tirelessly these two years, rarely missing class, utilizing every extra credit assignment I could, using every resource UHD offers as an opportunity to reach the top. As this day finally ends, as I type the final page of this book, I go to sleep knowing that a new door is waiting to open in the morning.

I ended my commencement speech with a message for the crowd, "The three messages I pray I sent my children today are, "Do what I do, not what I say," "Let me show you the way, not just tell you to do it," and "I will not ask you to do, what I am not willing to do with you." I say to each of you, "Do what you do the very best you can do it, find happiness in doing what is right and live your life with pride, knowing that it was the best you had to offer. I will awake in the morning to say once again, "Today is the first day of the rest of my life," and to you I say . . .

Now go find your door of success and I will see you at the top

The Door is Wide Open!